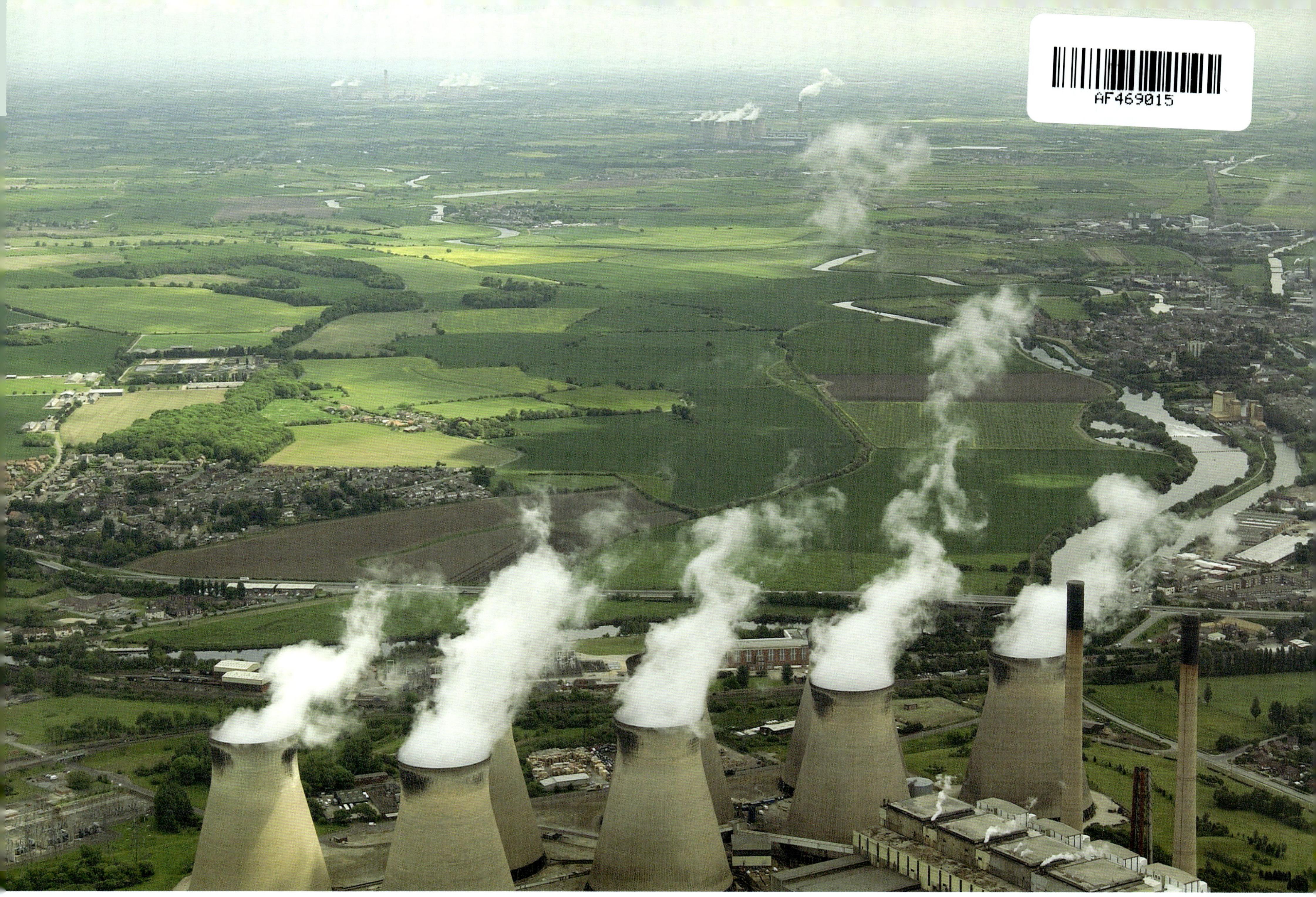

WEST YORKSHIRE
FROM ABOVE

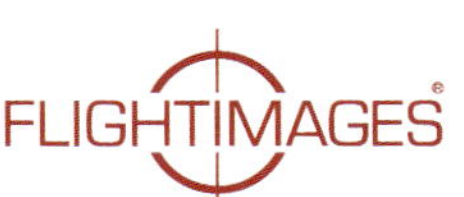

Photographs: IAN HAY, FLIGHT IMAGES
Text: MELVYN JONES

MYRIAD BOOKS

Leeds

Leeds, as *Loidis*, was first mentioned by the Venerable Bede in the early 8th century. It was given borough status by the lord of the manor, Maurice Paynel, in 1207. It thrived as a market town for hundreds of years, the original cloth market being held on Leeds Bridge. Daniel Defoe, in the 1720s, described it as "wealthy and populous" and said that its cloth market was "not to be equalled in the world". It was the development of water and rail transport that transformed Leeds into an industrial giant. In 1699 an Act was passed to create the Aire and Calder Navigation and in 1816 the Leeds and Liverpool Canal was completed. The first railway was the Leeds to Selby line which was opened in 1834 (linking the town to Hull), and in 1842 the Midland railway to London was opened, closely followed by the Leeds and Bradford railway and the Manchester and Leeds railway. Leeds became not only an important woollen cloth manufacturing centre but also a centre for the production of earthenware and a wide variety of engineering products including textile machinery. Today it is well-served by motorways (M1, M62 and A1M) and Leeds Bradford Airport. It is the commercial and financial metropolis of Yorkshire.

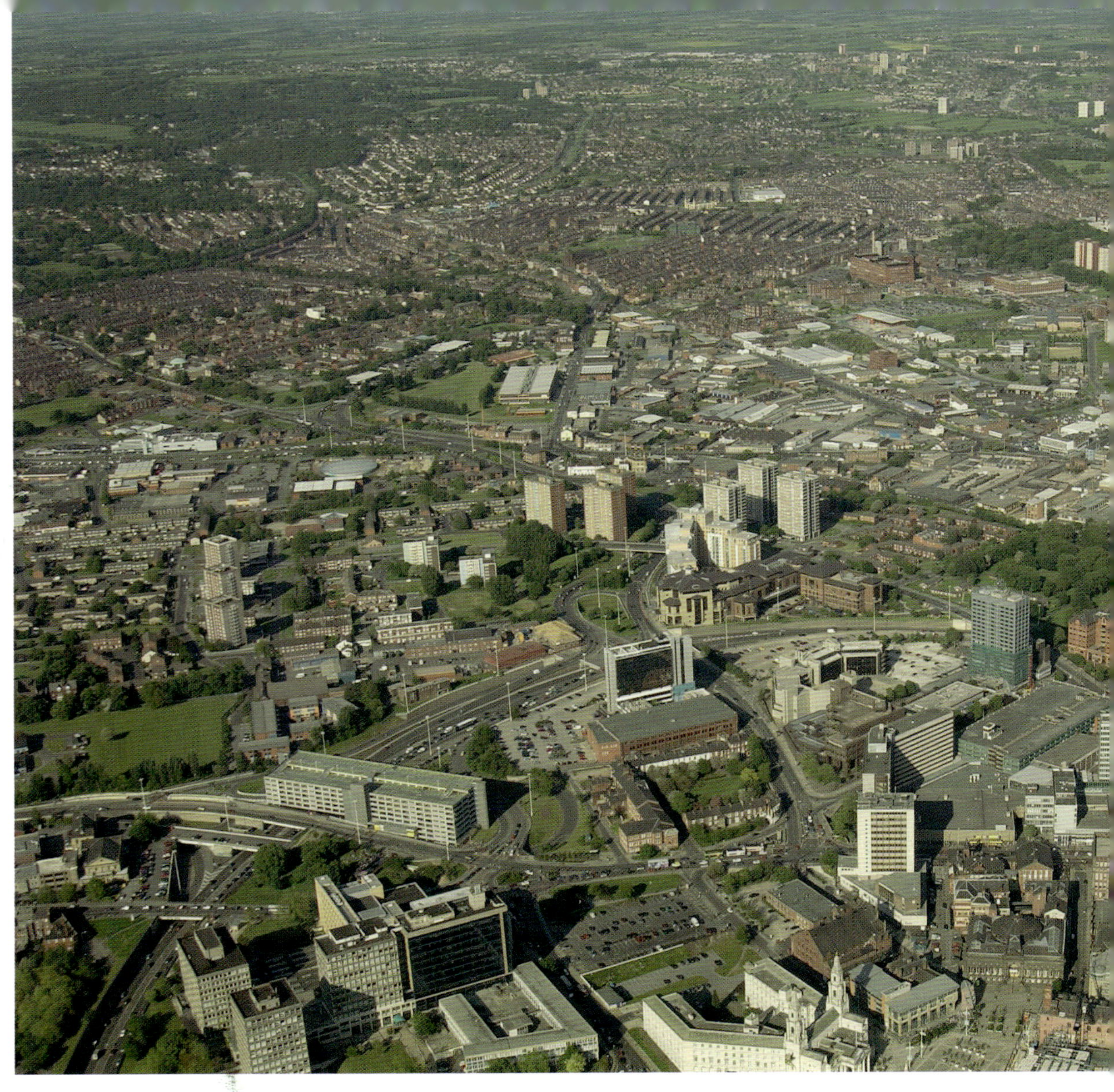

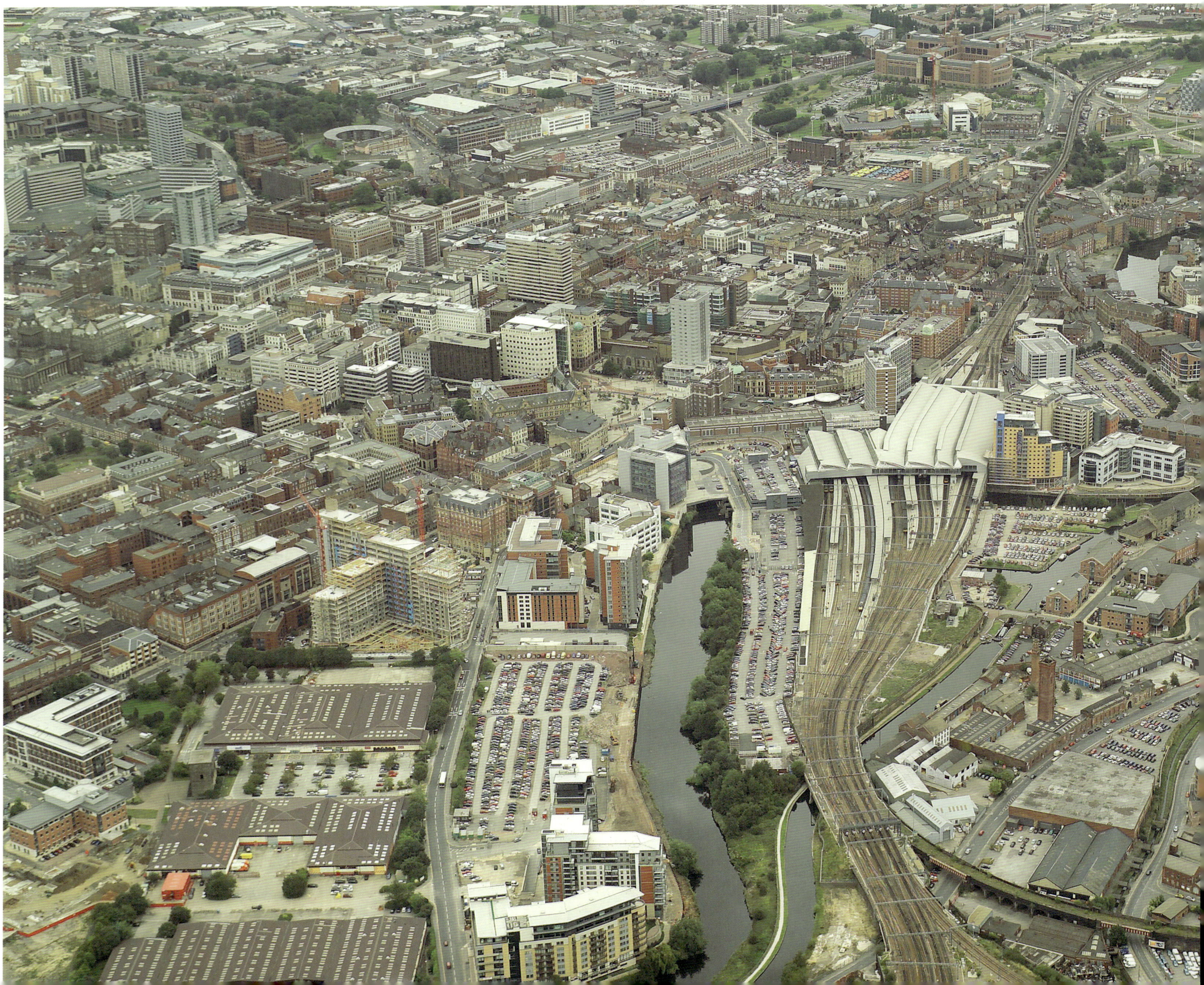

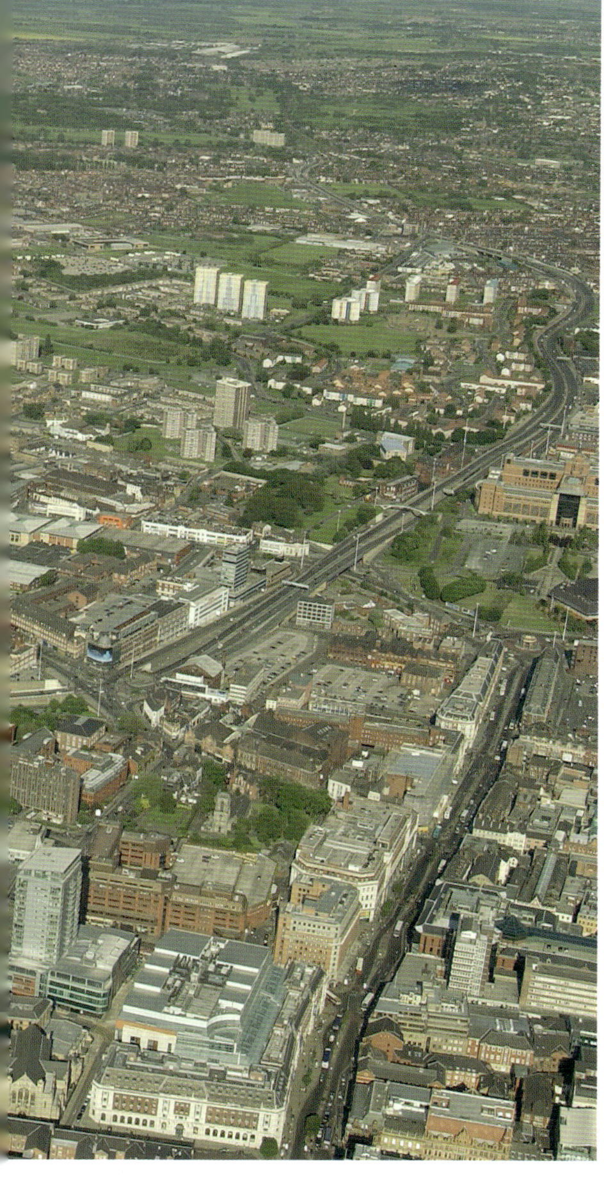

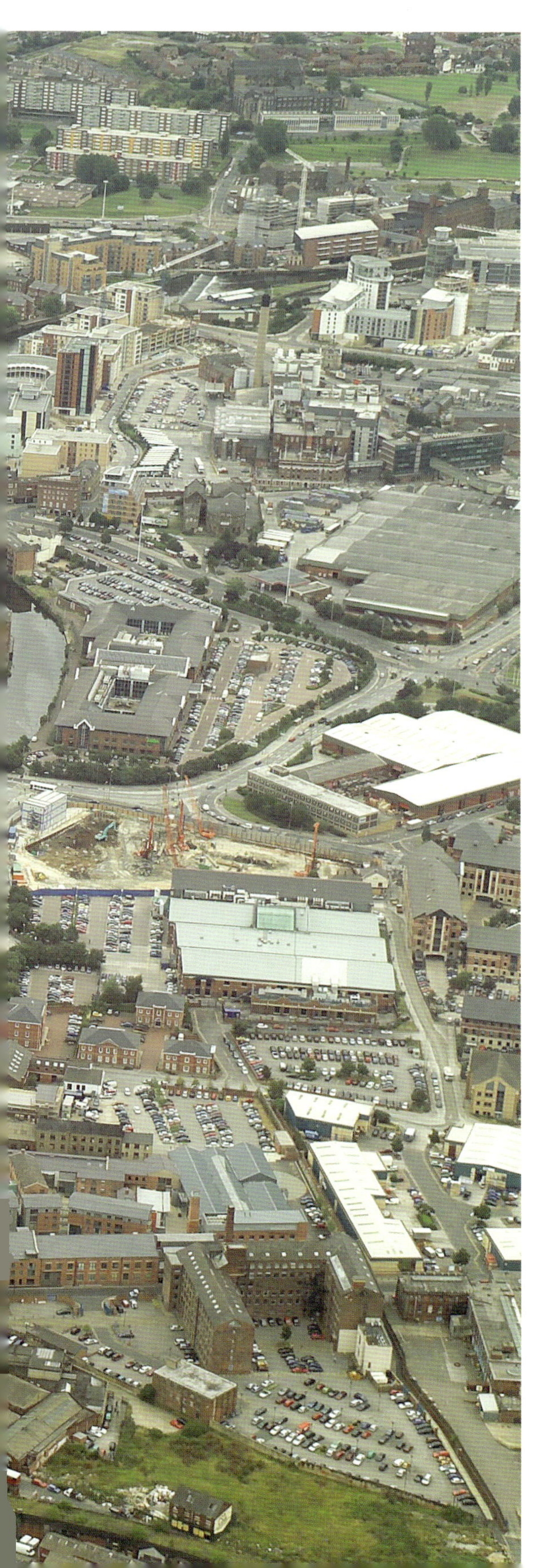

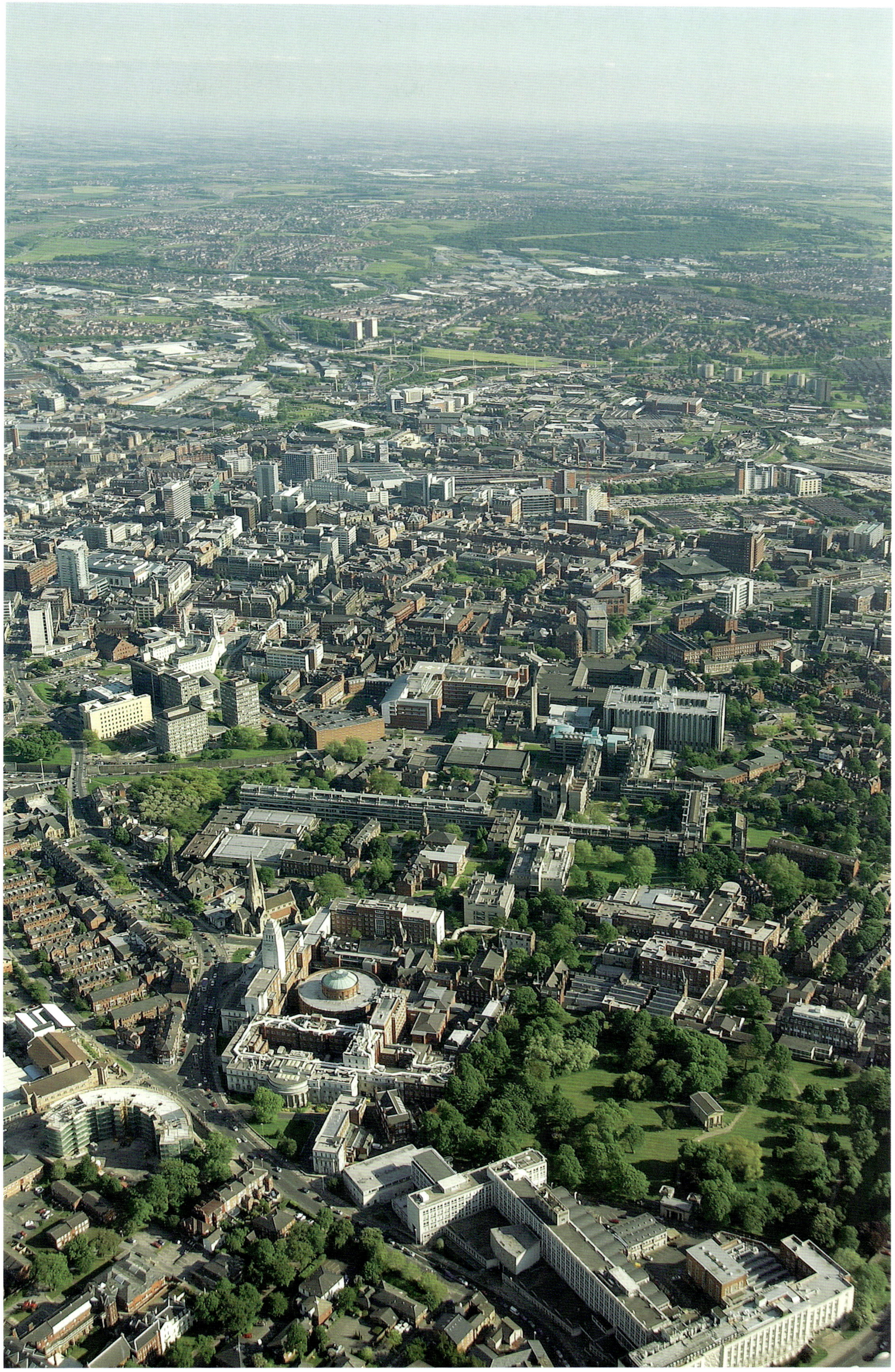

THREE VIEWS OF LEEDS

The photograph on the left shows the city from the west. In the foreground are the river Aire (on the left) and the Leeds and Liverpool Canal and Canal Wharf (on the right) separated by the railway lines running into Leeds City railway station. Leeds City Station came into being as late as 1938, as an amalgamation of the pre-existing New Station and Wellington Station. The new Queens Hotel which fronts the station on City Square was re-built at the same time to replace a Victorian hotel of the same name. The station was virtually re-built in 1960. The photograph above left is also a view from the west along The Headrow (bottom right) with the twin towers of the Civic Hall in the centre foreground looking towards Sheepscar, Chapeltown, Harehills and beyond. The photograph above is from the north looking over the campus of the University of Leeds with the prominent tower of the Parkinson Building, built in 1926. This university (there is another, Leeds Metropolitan University) was originally the Yorkshire College of Science, then the Victoria University in 1887 and the University of Leeds in 1904. Beyond the university is the city centre and beyond that the City Station and the suburbs of Hunslet and Beeston to the south of the river Aire.

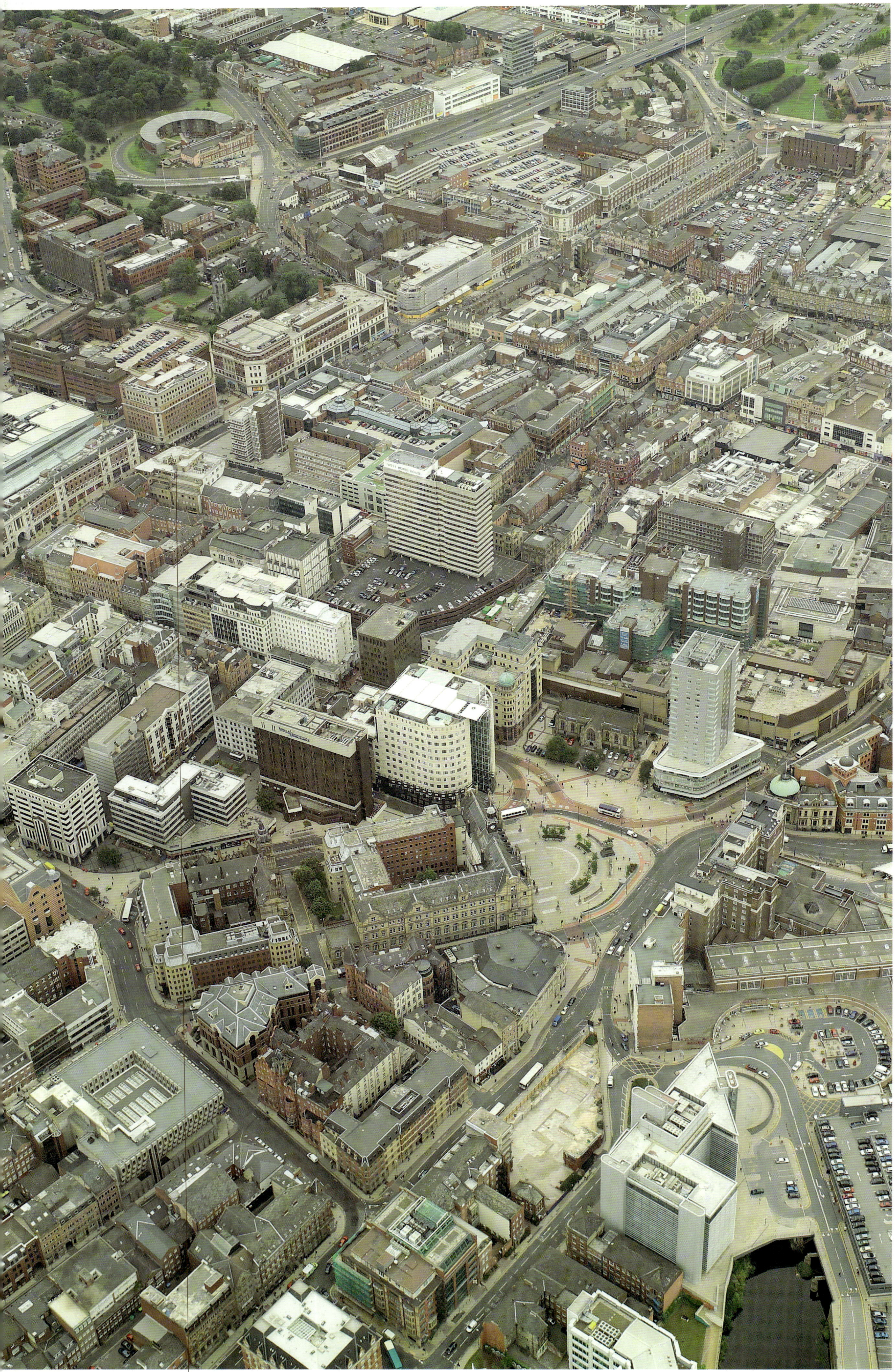

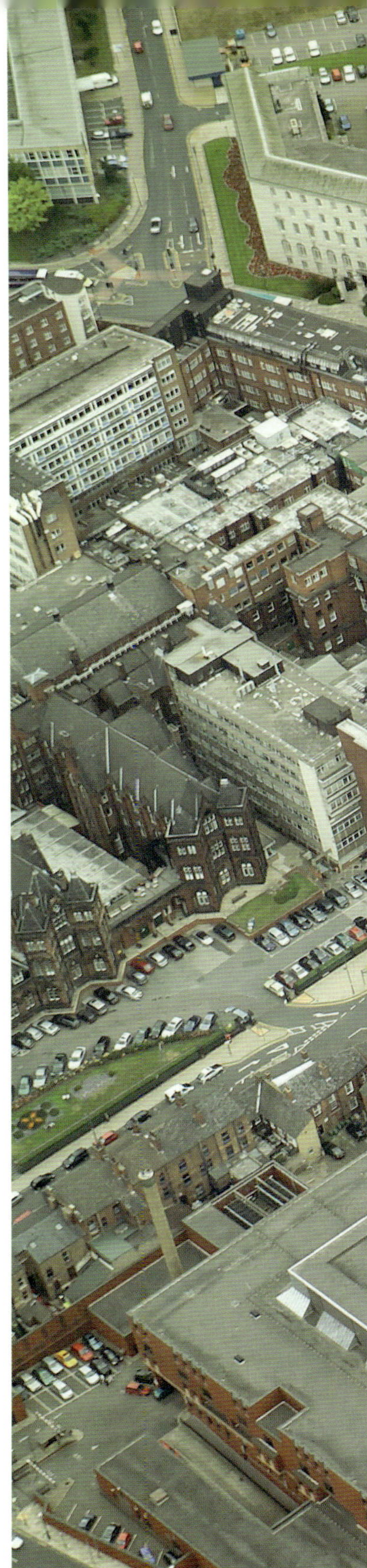

LEEDS CITY CENTRE

As the three photographs on these two pages show, Leeds has a "big city" townscape. On the left the view is over City Square outside the City Station looking eastwards with the river Aire in the foreground. The large square building with its central turret overlooking the western edge of the square is the General Post Office building built in 1896. The grid-iron street layout to the east of the square has The Headrow at the top left running away towards the roundabout on the A61 with the main junction formed where the The Headrow is crossed by Briggate. Beyond Briggate at the junction of Vicar Lane and Kirkgate stands the Baroque exterior of the City Markets (Kirkgate Market). In the streets between City Square and Vicar Lane are the famous shopping arcades of central Leeds.

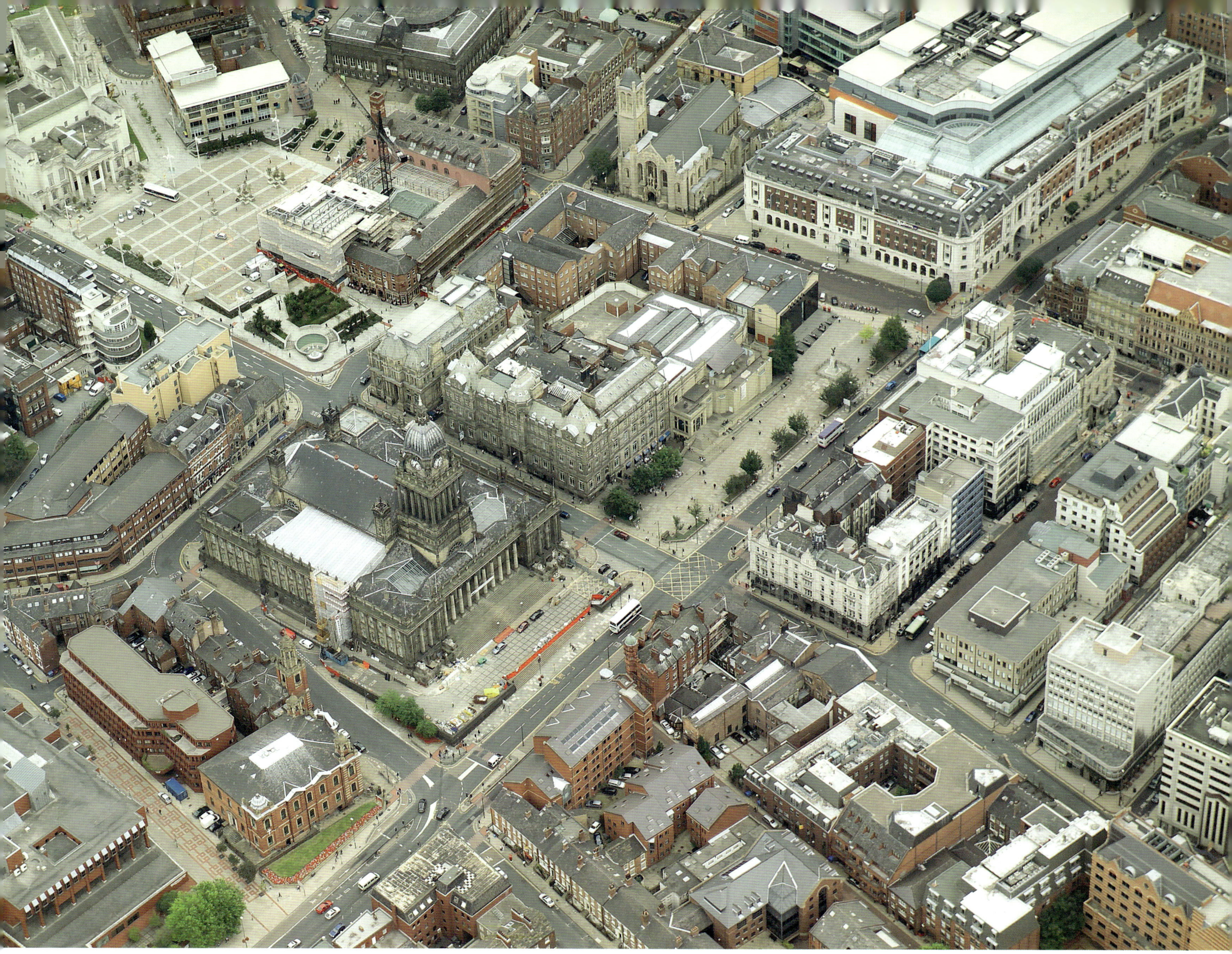

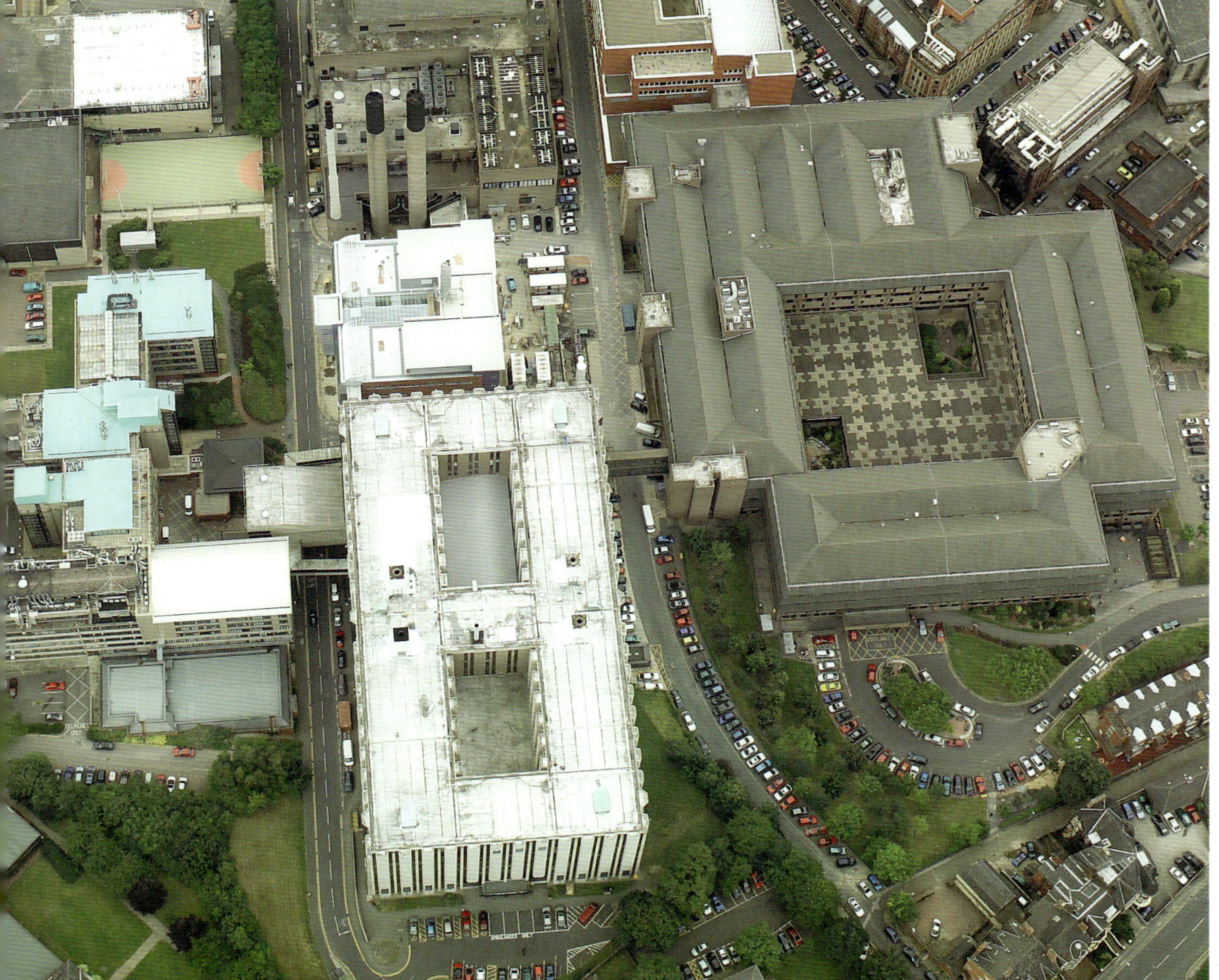

THE HEADROW *(above)*

The Headrow, which runs from the bottom-left to top-right across the photograph was the main east-west route through early Leeds. It was widened by Leeds town planners between 1928-32 creating the wide modern street. It is the civic and commercial heart of the city. Dominating the centre of the photograph is Leeds Town Hall, constructed between 1853-58 and designed by Cuthbert Brodrick, the Hull architect. It is a solid and confident flagship of a proud Victorian city on the move. The building is topped by a magnificent domed clock tower rising to 225ft (68m). Beside the town hall, across Calverley Street also facing The Headrow, are the Municipal Buildings designed in 1876 by George Carson, now housing the city's Museum and Central Library. Beyond the Municipal Buildings still on the north side of the Headrow is the former Leeds Permanent Building Society building (Permanent House), now "The Light" and containing shops, bars and a hotel. Behind The Light, on Cookridge Street, is the Roman Catholic Cathedral dating from 1902-04. At the top of the photograph beyond Centenary Square is the Civic Hall with its twin towers dating from 1933. Finally, of great architectural and social interest, are the town houses in Park Square East, across The Headrow opposite the western side of the Town Hall. Begun in 1778 and completed in 1794, Park Square is the only Georgian residential square in Leeds and was once the home of gentlemen, lawyers, merchants and surgeons.

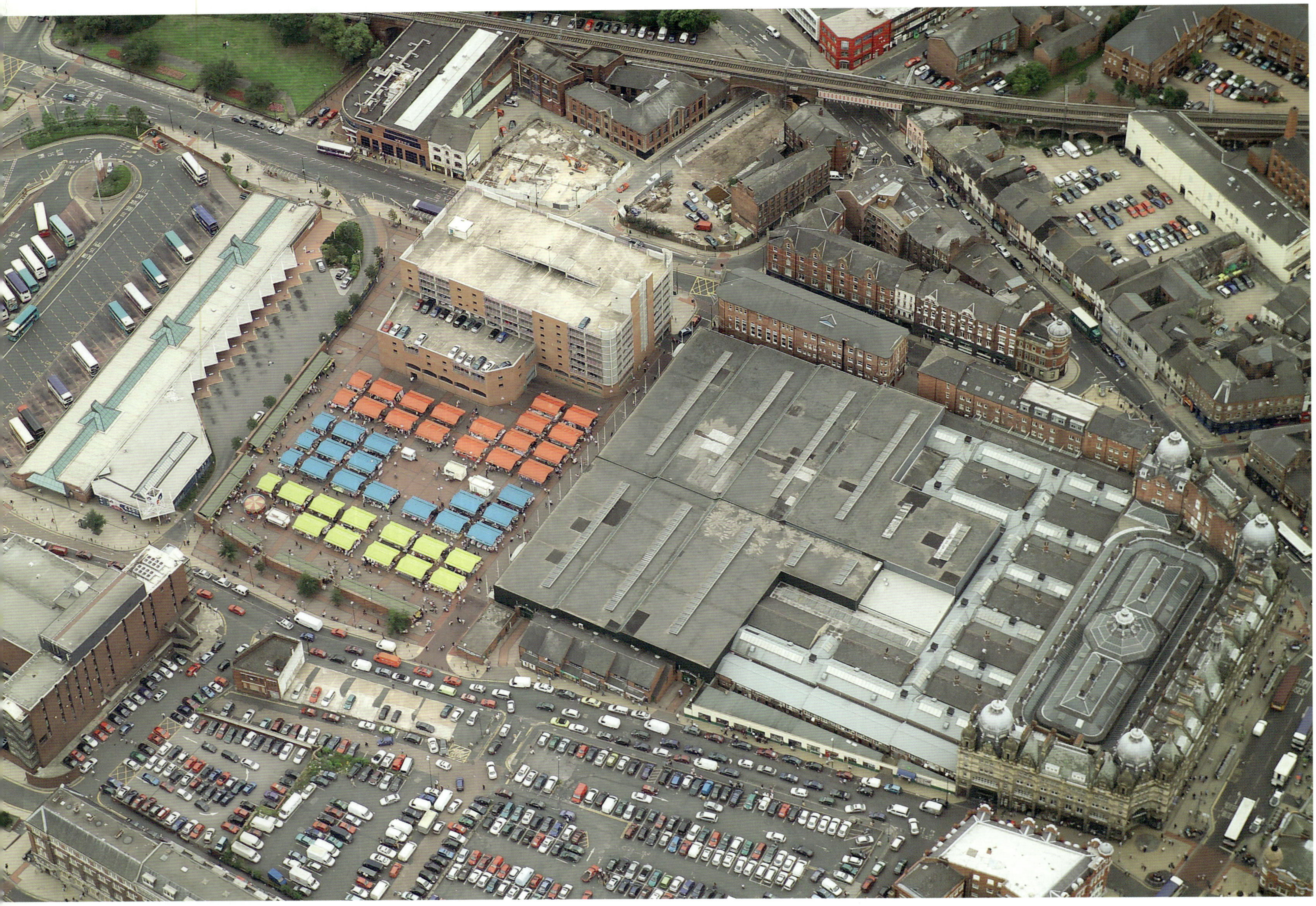

KIRKGATE MARKET

(above)

The original market hall was built in 1857 in the Crystal Palace style on land previously occupied by the open Free Market at the junction of Kirkgate and Vicar Lane. This was replaced by a new market hall in 1904 by architects John and Joseph Leeming. A disastrous fire in 1975 destroyed two-thirds of the interior and another fire in 1992 set back restoration work that had begun in 1991. Now the exterior stonework has been repaired, the domes rebuilt and shop units and stalls replaced or repaired in their original style. Other surrounding Victorian market buildings have been restored and the open market has been provided with new stalls and a central market square created.

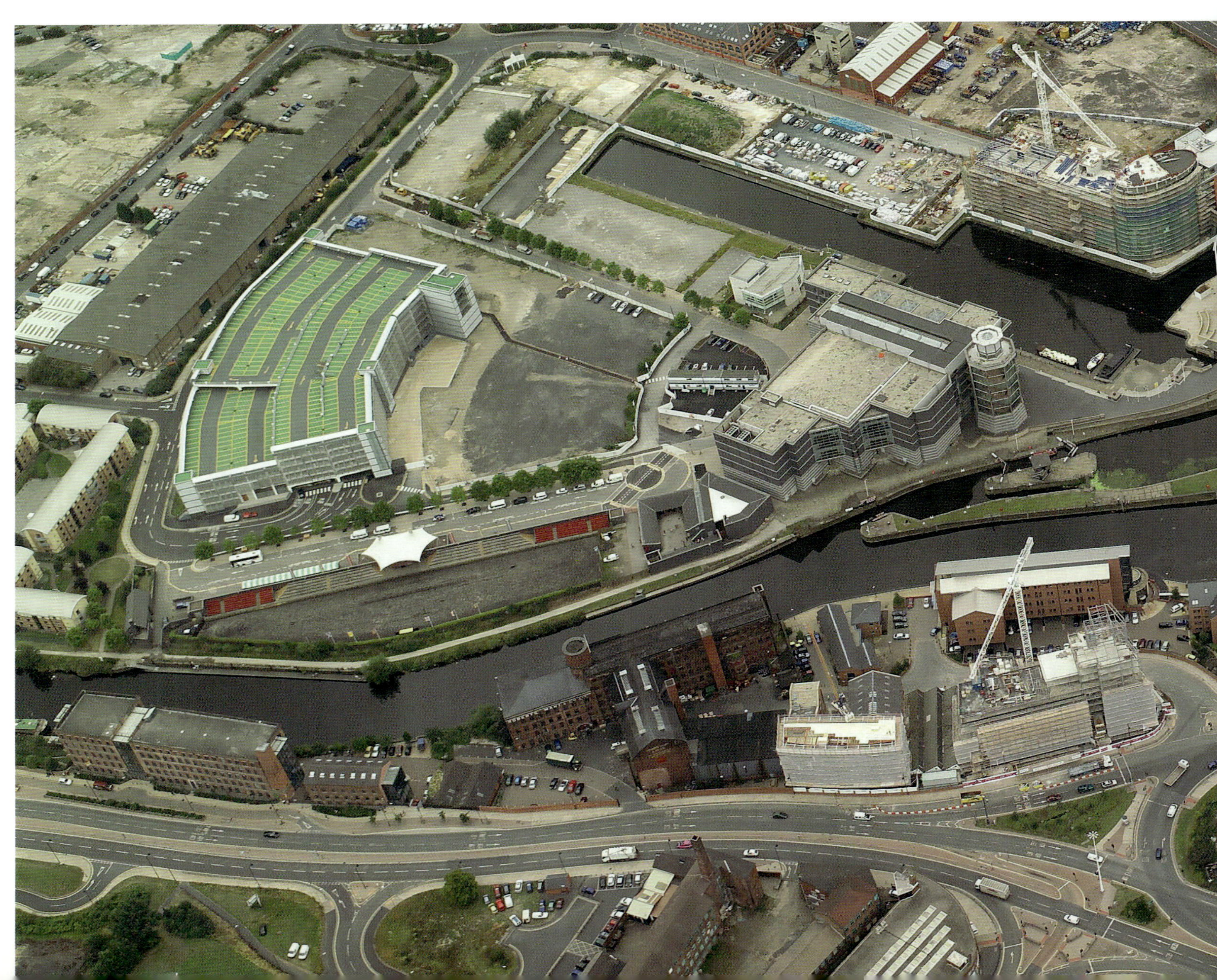

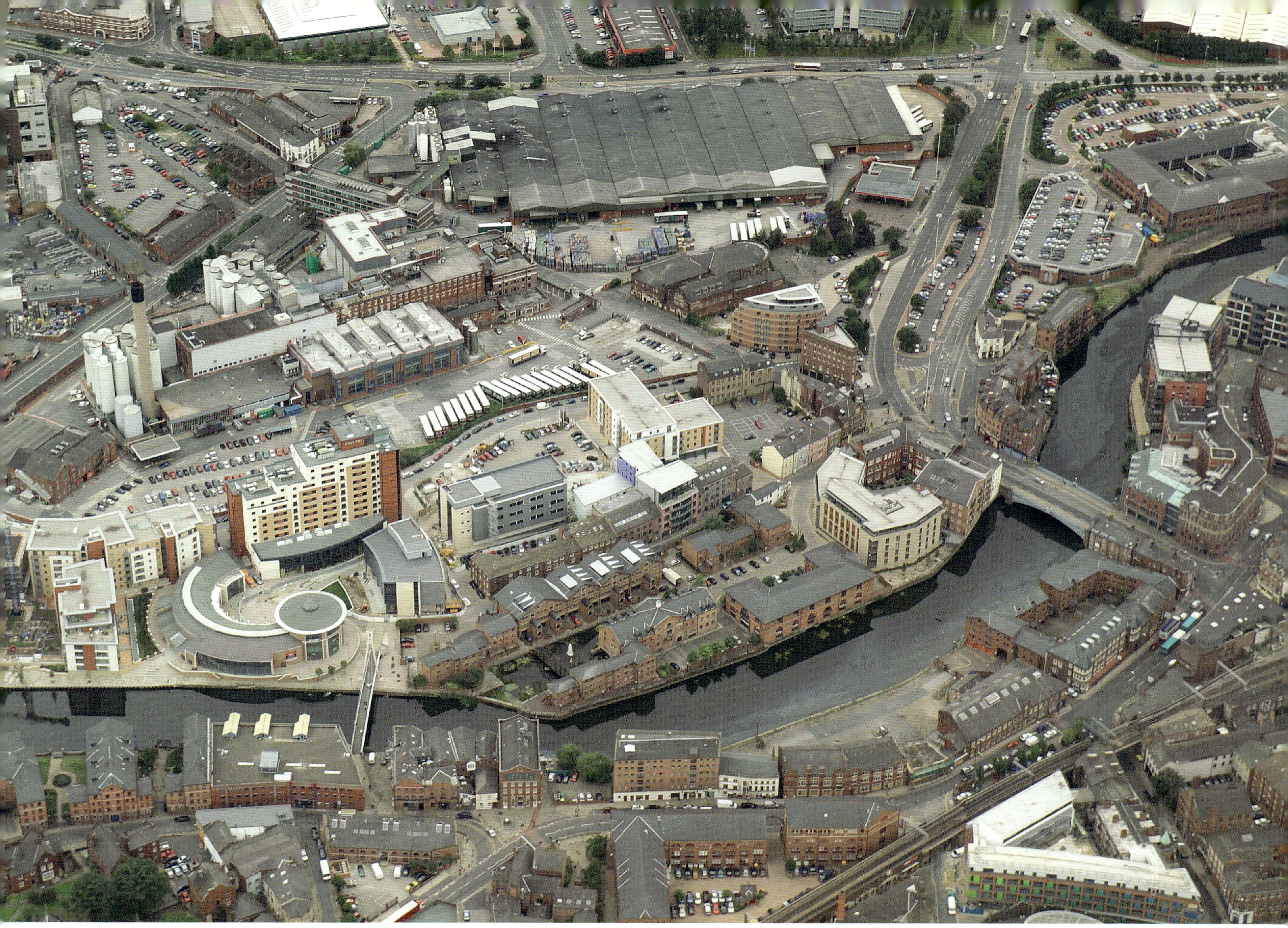

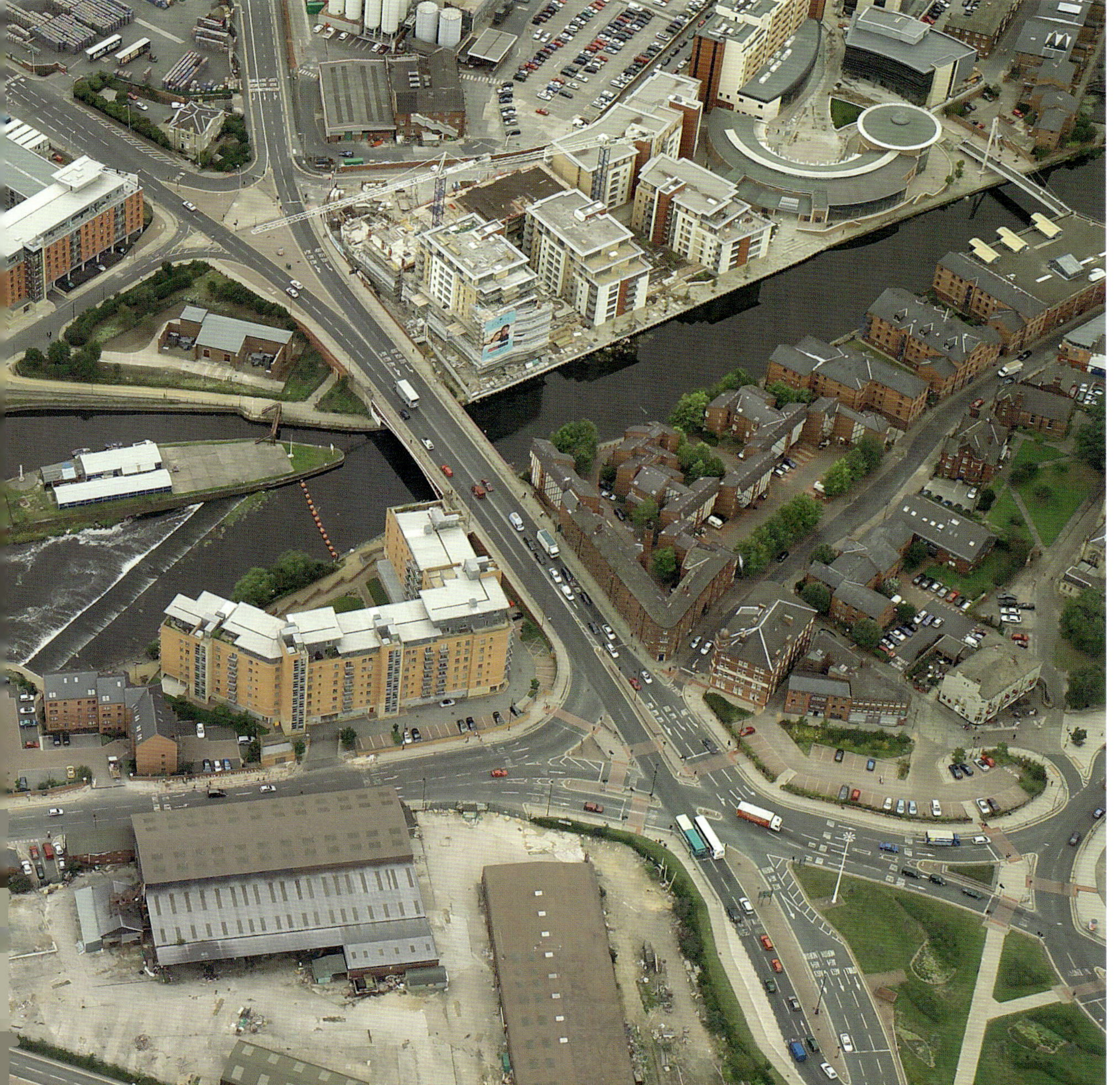

LEEDS WATERFRONT *(left & above)*

This was Leeds' dockland area at the termini of the Aire and Calder Navigation and the Leeds and Liverpool Canal. By the 1960s this area was rundown and partially derelict. It has now been transformed, primarily through the enterprise of the Leeds Development Corporation working with both the City Council and the private sector. Existing warehouses have been converted into apartments and offices and new riverside apartments and office buildings have been constructed.

The photograph above shows the waterfront from the north with Leeds Bridge leading to Briggate (towards the bottom of the photograph) and the new development at Brewery Wharf on the south side of the river Aire (bottom left) with its high-quality office space, hotel, cafes, bars, restaurants and 360 apartments.

In the photograph to the immediate left a crane still towers over new building beside Clarence Dock on the river Aire in this revived area of waterfront to the south-east of the old city centre. The new building is a £200m mixed-use development which includes apartments, offices, shops and leisure outlets sited around the dock area. Pride of place, however, goes to the Royal Armouries Museum which relocated from London to Leeds and opened in 1996 between the dock and the river. This national museum of arms and armour has 5,000 objects on permanent display with five themed galleries on War, Tournament, Self Defence, Hunting and Arms and Armour of the Orient.

HOLBECK & HUNSLET *(right)*

This long view over southern Leeds from the north-west covers Holbeck (right foreground) and Hunslet in the background. Both Holbeck and Hunslet today are industrial as well as residential suburbs with a mixture of old industrial buildings, modern industrial estates and terraces, villas and high rise blocks. Holbeck was where the famous engineer Matthew Murray (1765-1826) set up his foundry at Mill Green in 1795 and his new works, the New Foundry, at Water Lane in 1802. Murray made his first steam engine in 1799, was the first to make machine tools and in 1812 made the first commercially successful steam locomotive for the Middleton Colliery a few miles to the south. This locomotive did the work previously undertaken by 50 horses and 200 men. A painting of one of Murray's locomotives at Middleton Colliery is famously featured in George Walker's *Costumes of Yorkshire* in 1814. Murray lived at Holbeck Lodge or "Steam Hall", probably the first domestic dwelling in the world heated by steam! Holbeck was transformed in the 19th century from a pleasant village and surrounded by meadowland watered by the Hol Beck into an industrial suburb of Leeds based on its rapidly growing engineering works. The need for sound housing for its working population gave rise to the foundation of a succession of "Holbeck Societies", deliberately short-lived but very successful building societies, the first one founded in 1845. These early societies led to the foundation in 1875 of the Leeds and Holbeck Permanent Building Society, the word "Permanent" being removed from the name in 1929. The Society is still going strong today. Hunslet is the location of the famous Garden Gate Inn, a complete Edwardian public house surviving in the middle of a modern council estate with its original tilework, mosaics, intricate glasswork and joinery.

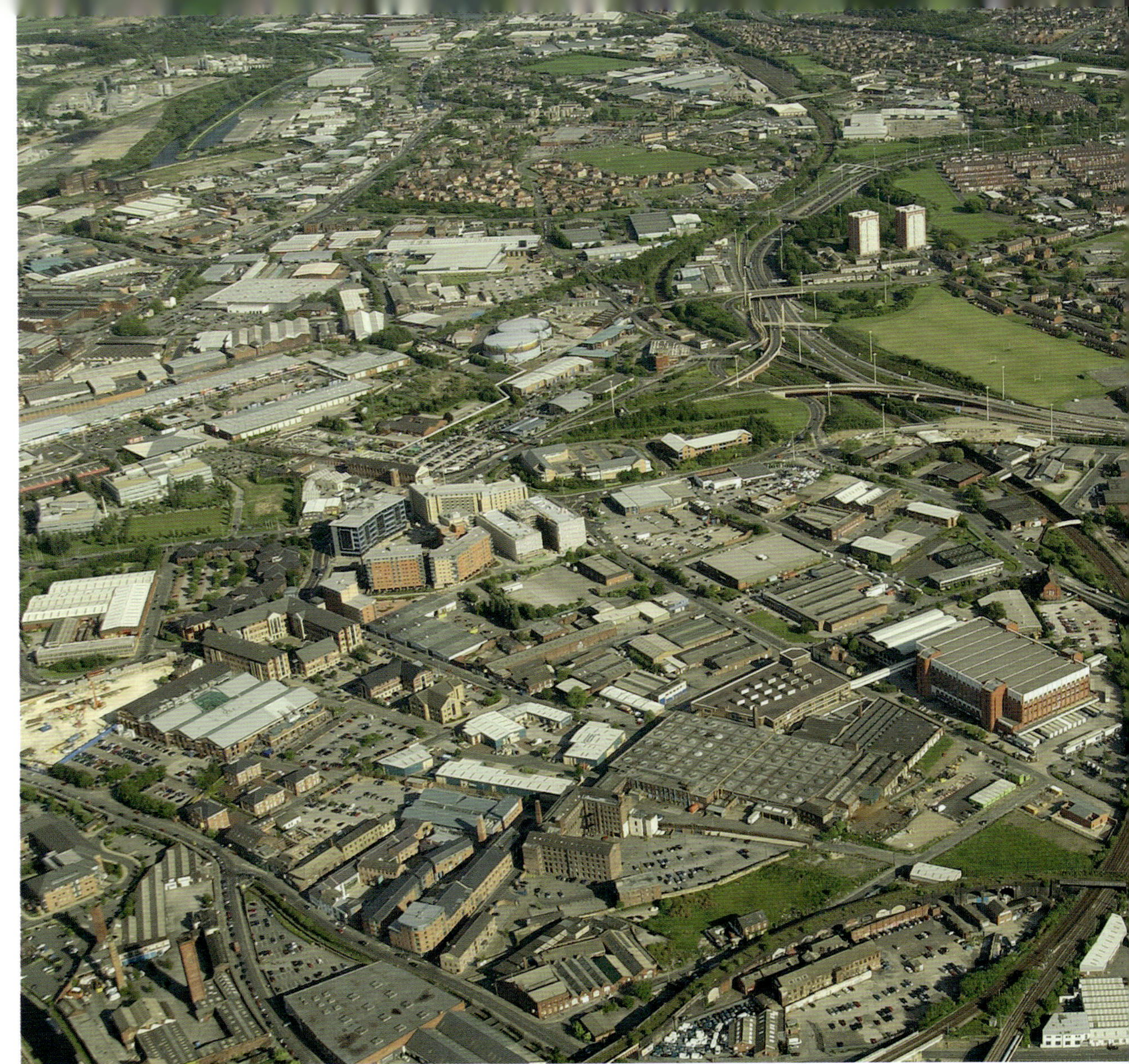

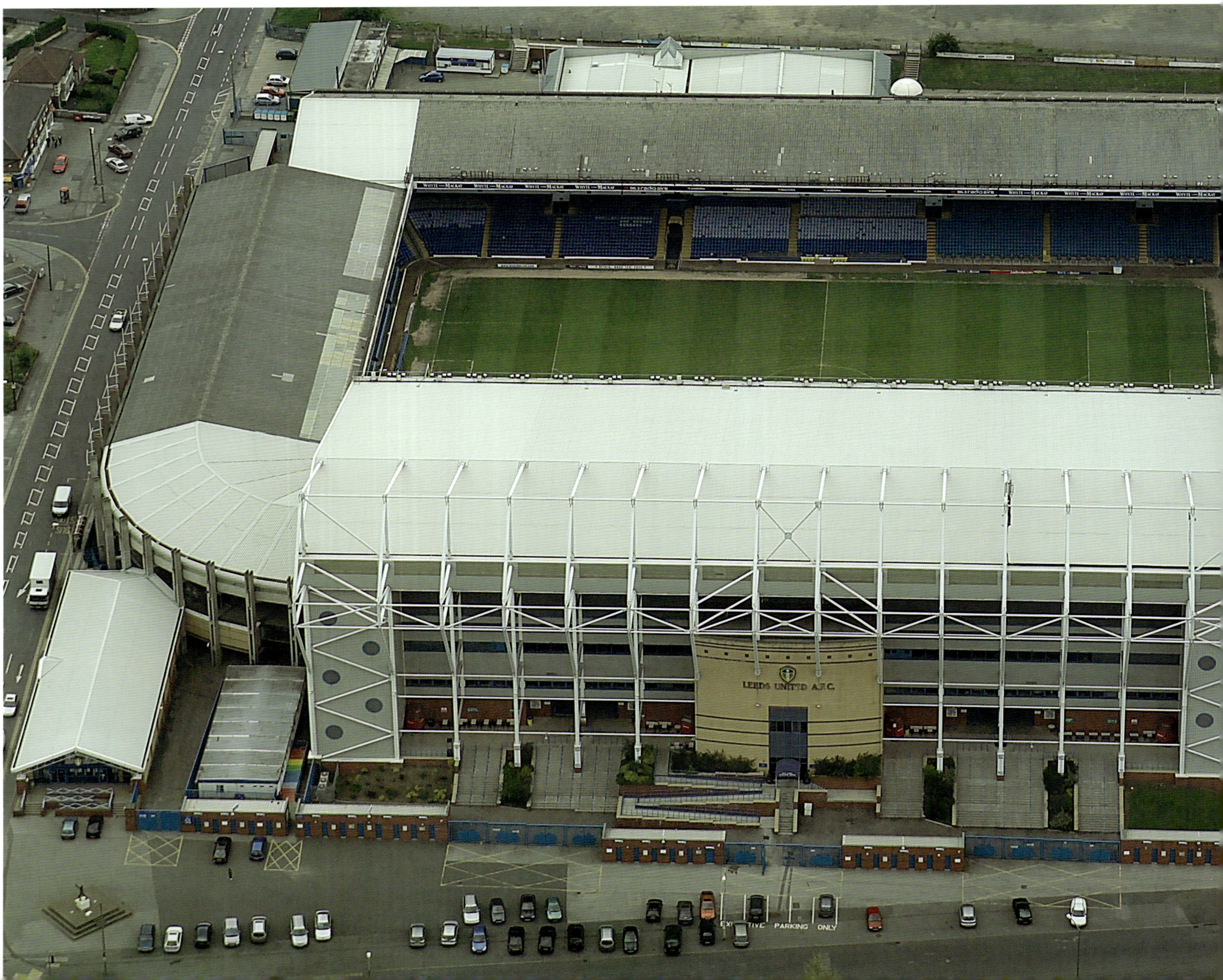

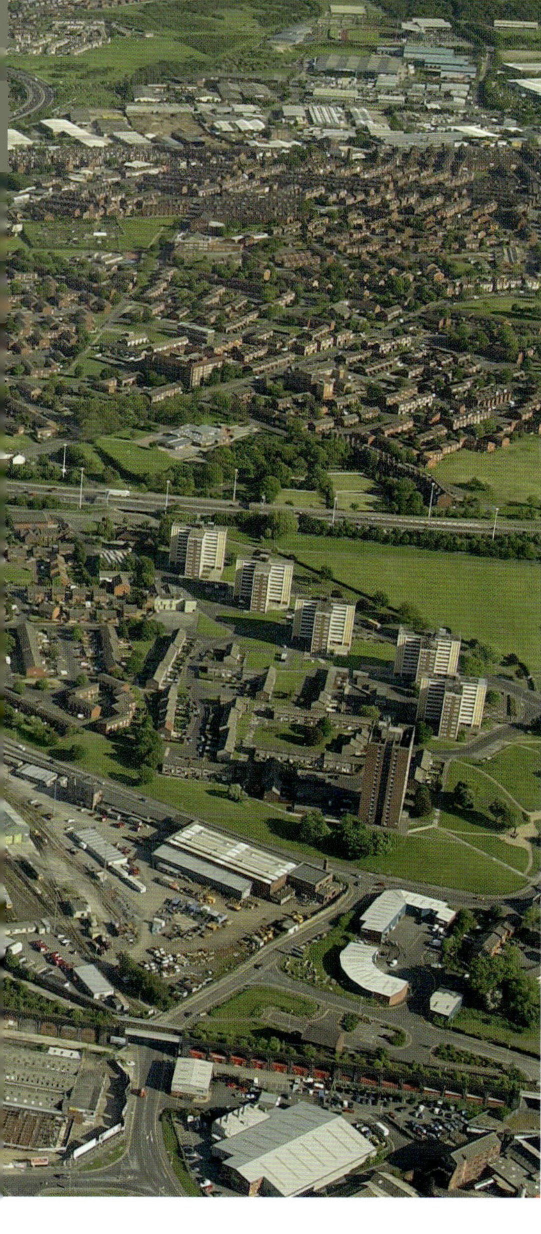

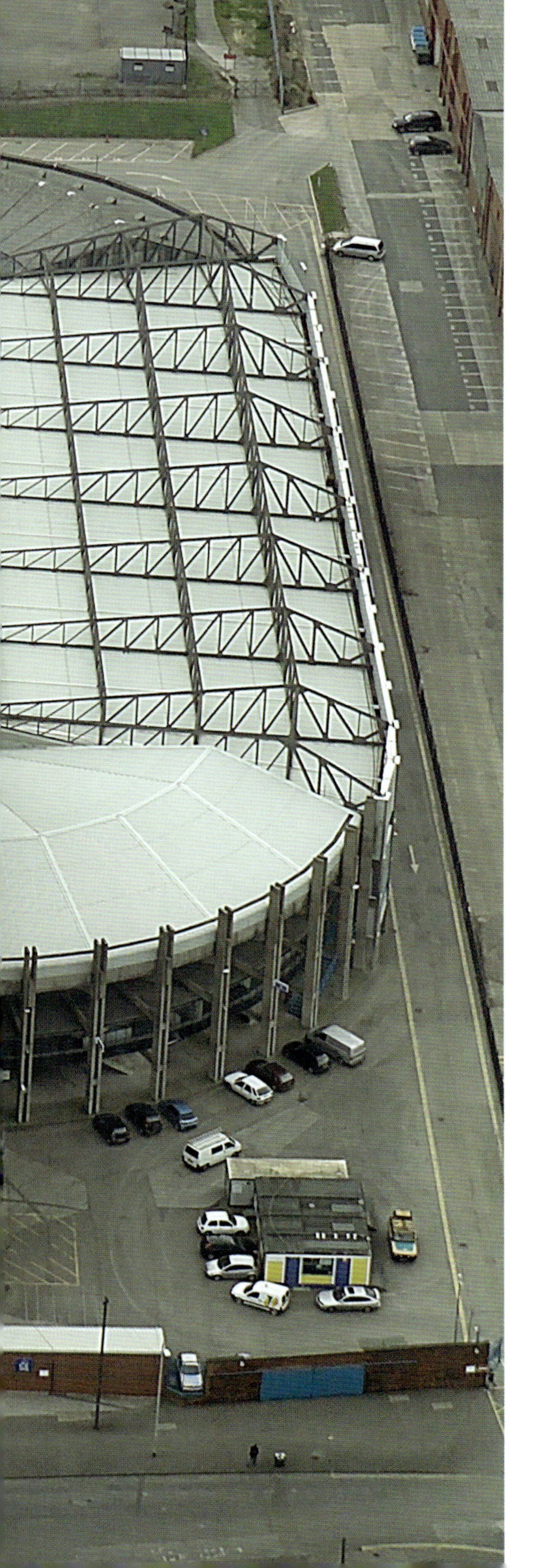

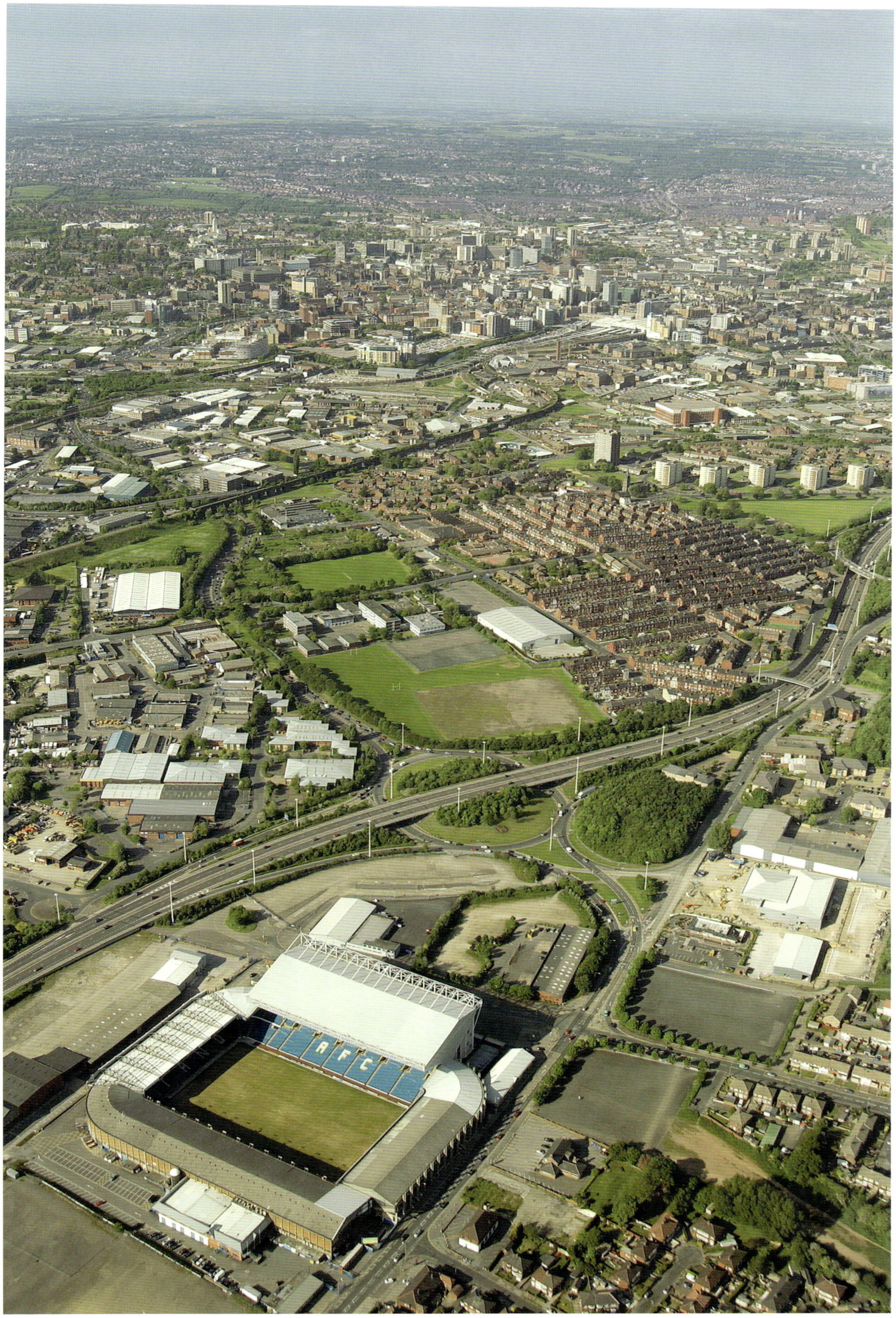

ELLAND ROAD *(above & left)*

Elland Road became the home of Leeds United Football Club following the ejection from the Football League of their predecessors, Leeds City, for making illegal payments to players. Leeds United were elected to the Football League in 1920. The development of the ground has gone through a number of important stages. The first stand, the West Stand, was built in the days of the Leeds City club in 1905 and this was followed in the 1920s by the so-called Scratching Shed and Spion Kop.

A new Kop (now the Don Revie Stand) was constructed in 1958 and in 1974 the Scratching Shed was replaced by the South Stand. The latest addition was the cantilever stand, the biggest in the world. The record attendance at the ground was 57,892 in a cup tie against Sunderland in March 1967. The modern ground capacity is just over 40,000. Leeds United won the First Division Championship in 1968, 1974 and 1993 and the FA Cup in 1972. The greatest period in the club's history came in the Don Revie era of the 1960s and early 1970s. During the period when Revie was manager (1961-74) the club won the First Division Championship twice, the FA Cup once, the League Cup once and the European Fairs Cup twice. The array of outstanding players at the club during that period was almost endless, including Billy Bremner, Jack Charlton, Johnny Giles, Eddie Gray, Peter Lorimer, Alan Clarke and Norman Hunter.

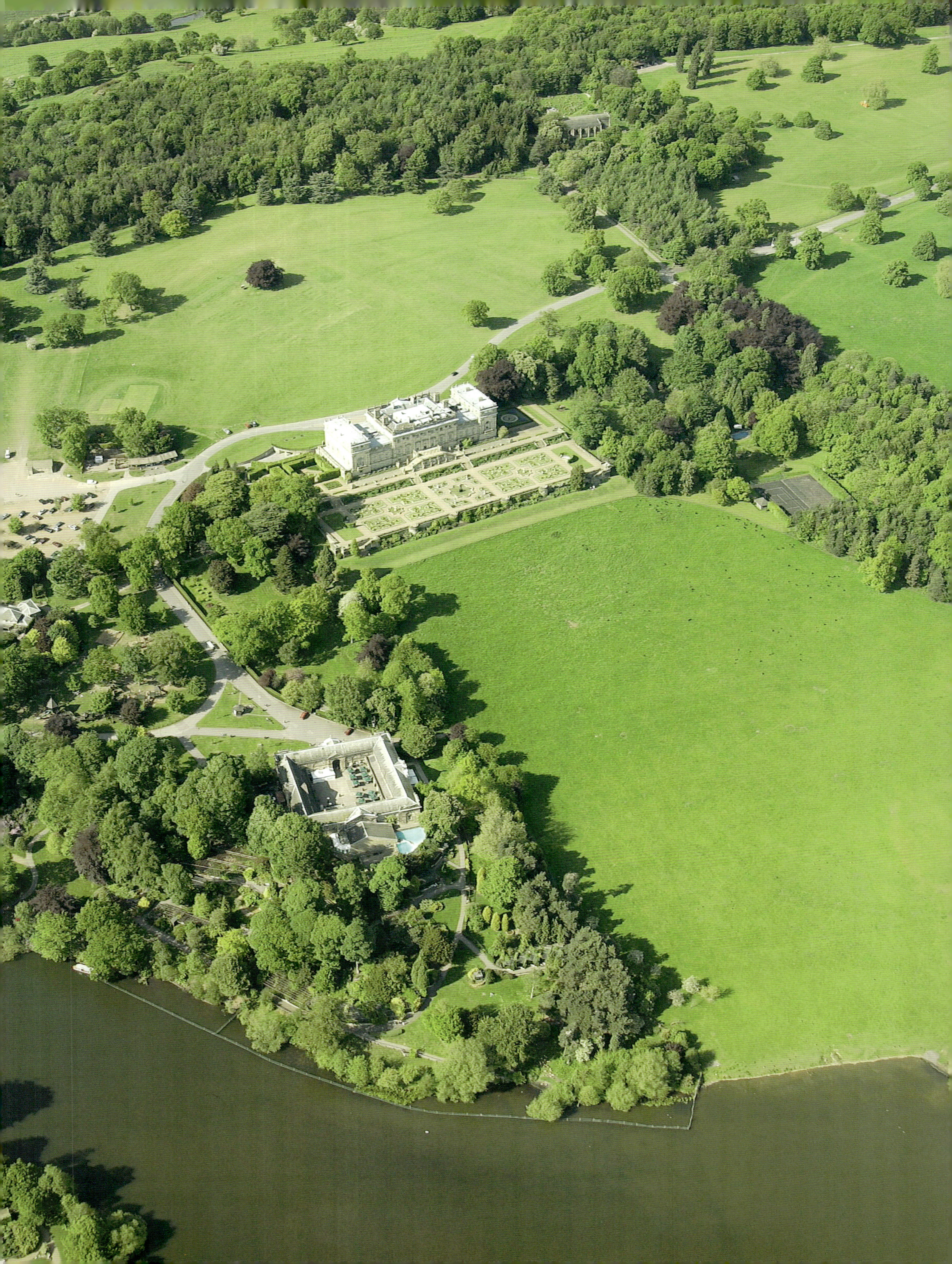

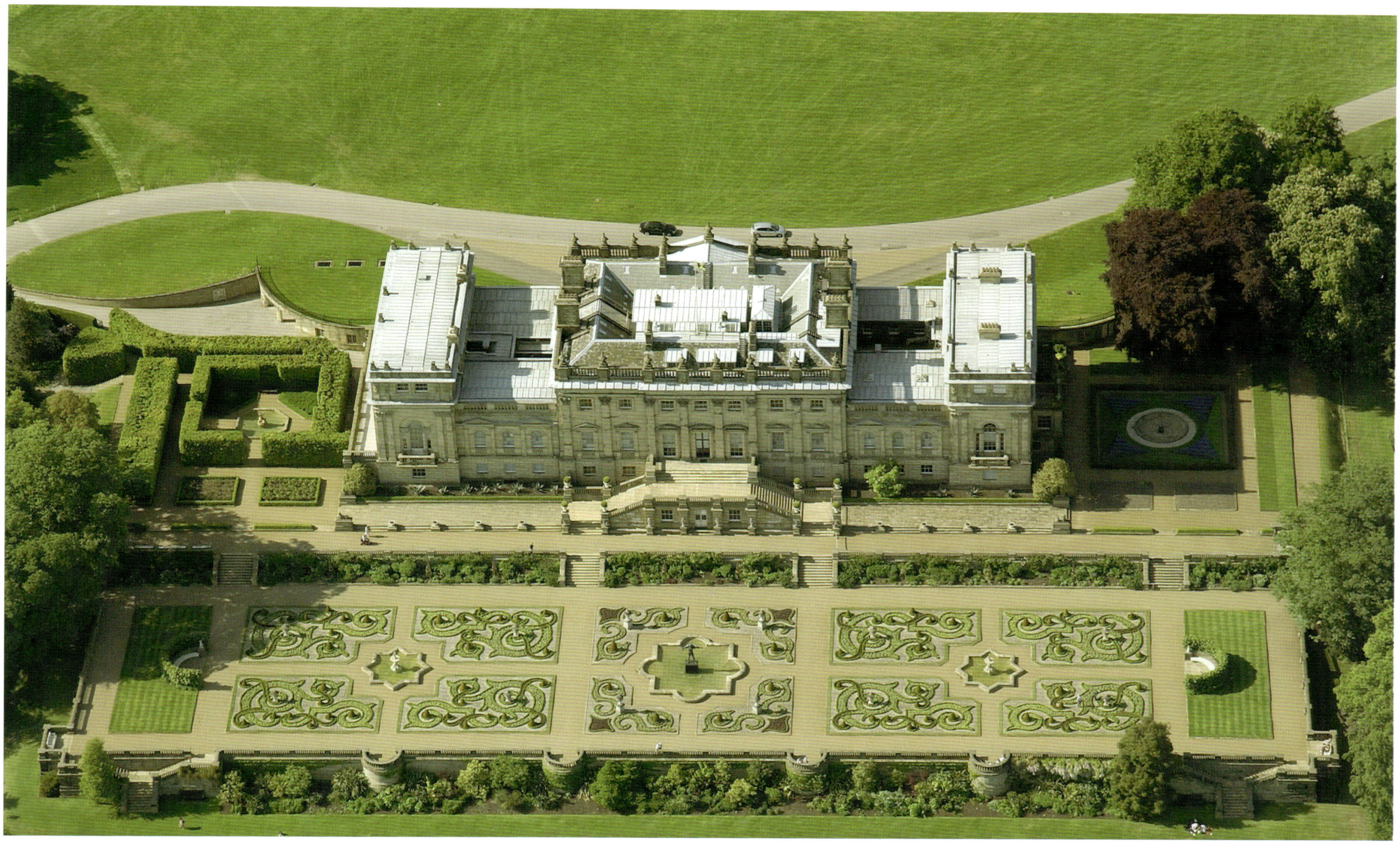

HAREWOOD HOUSE

This magnificent country house, the home of Earl and Countess Lascelles, was built by the York architect, John Carr, between 1759 and 1772 on the instructions of Edwin Lascelles whose father had made his fortune in the ribbon trade, from his position as collector of customs in Barbados and his directorship of the East India Company. The interiors were the work of Robert Adam and much of the furniture is documented work by Thomas Chippendale. In the 1840s the south facade of the house was remodelled by Sir Charles Barry, the architect of the Houses of Parliament. Immediately beyond the house to the south is an elaborate Italianate parterre with intricately-shaped flower beds, fountains and herbaceous borders. The grounds of the house, which include a serpentine lake, were laid out by Capability Brown.

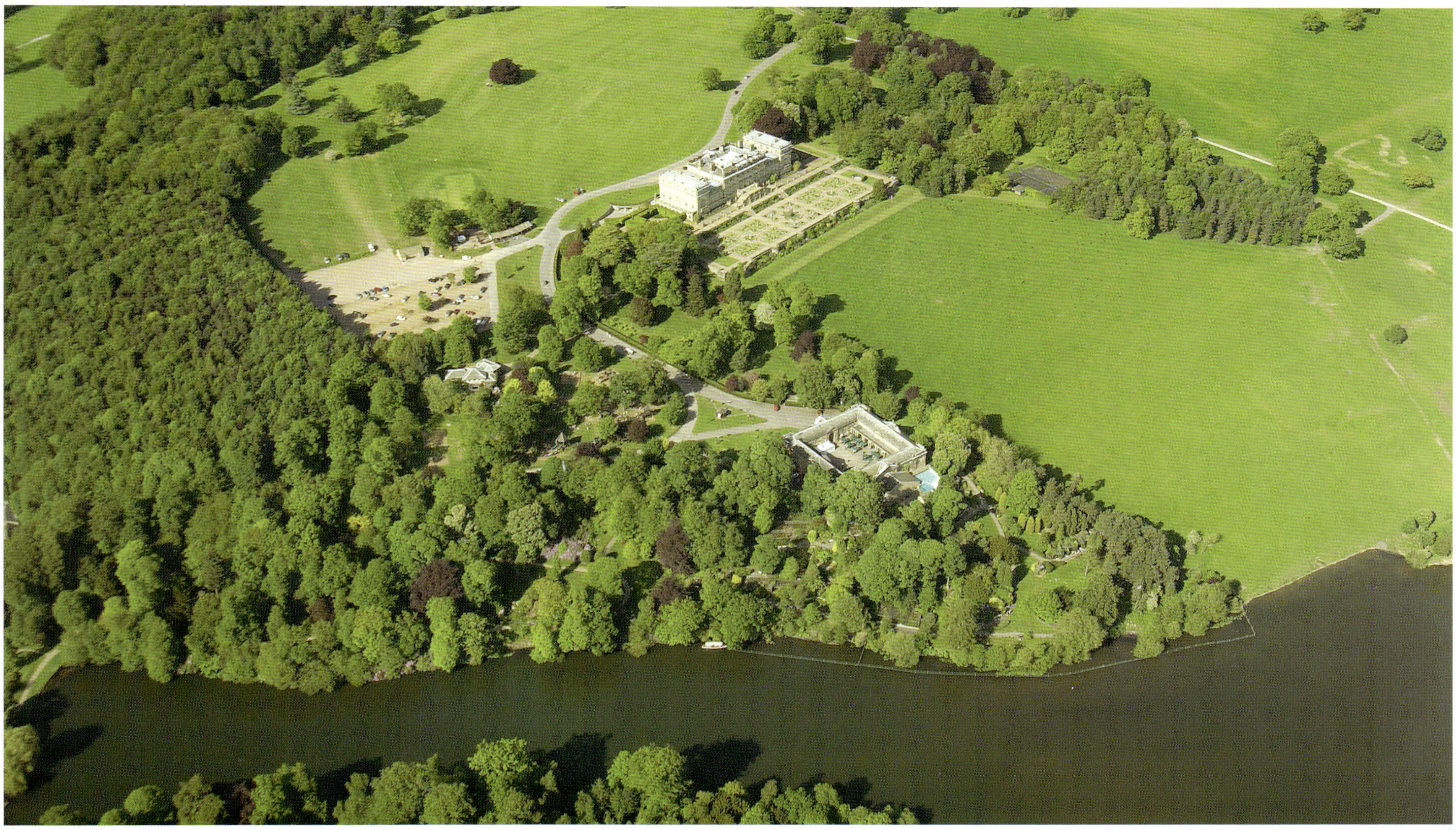

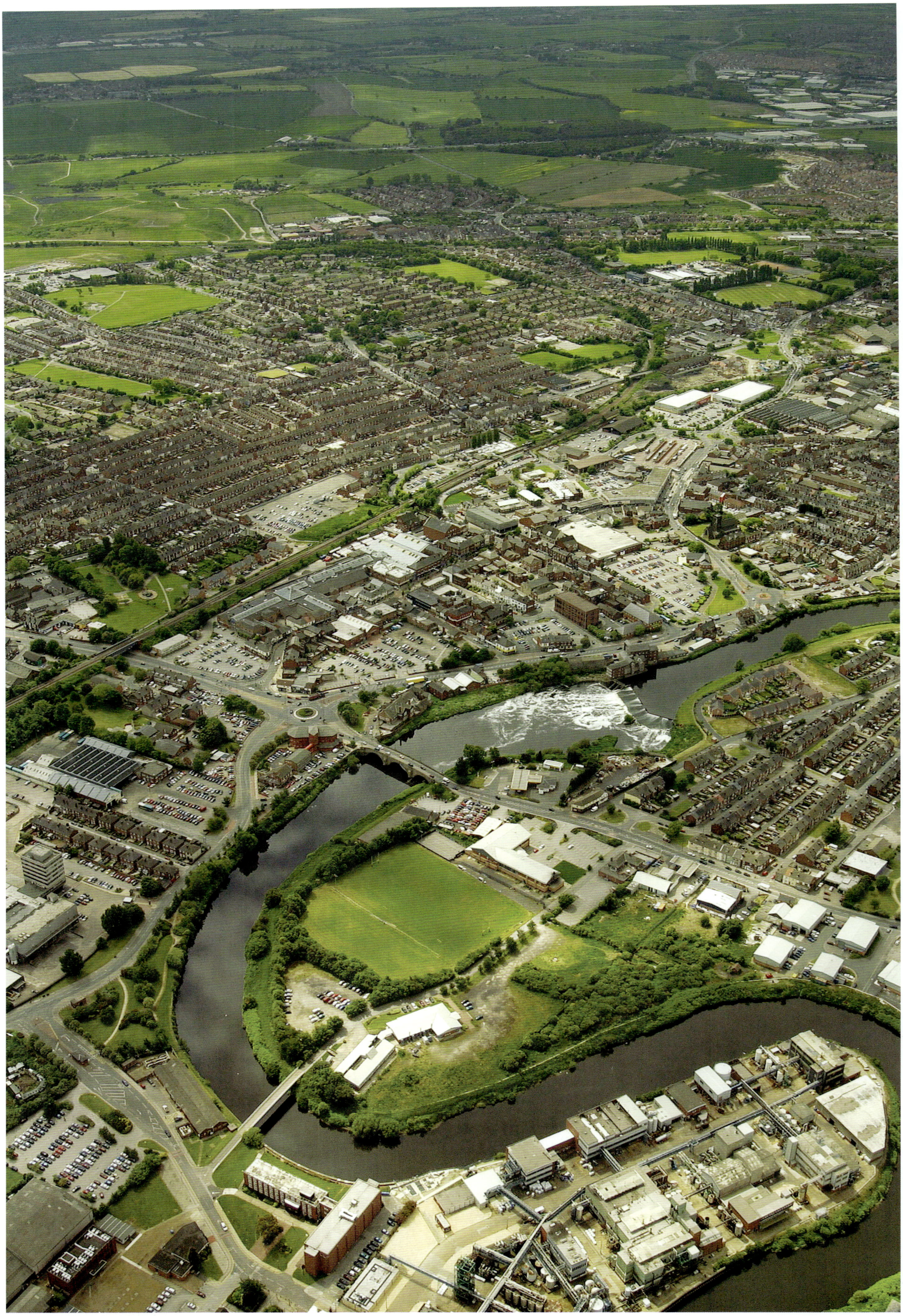

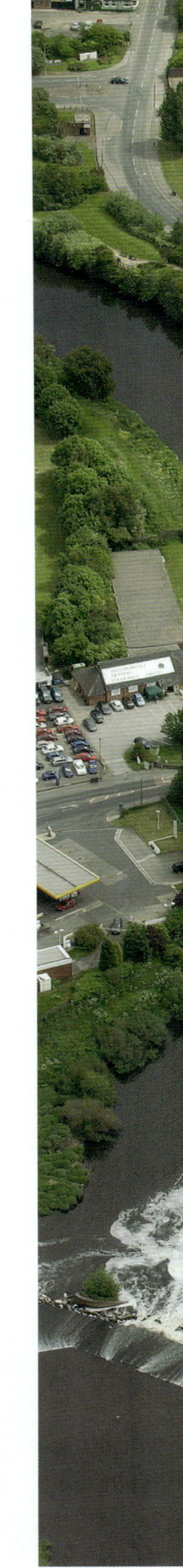

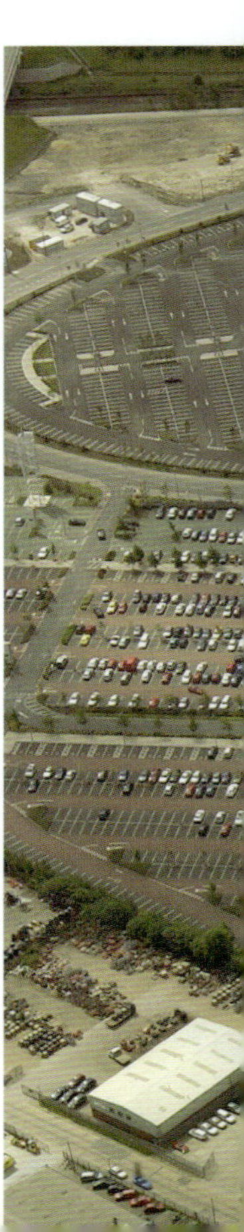

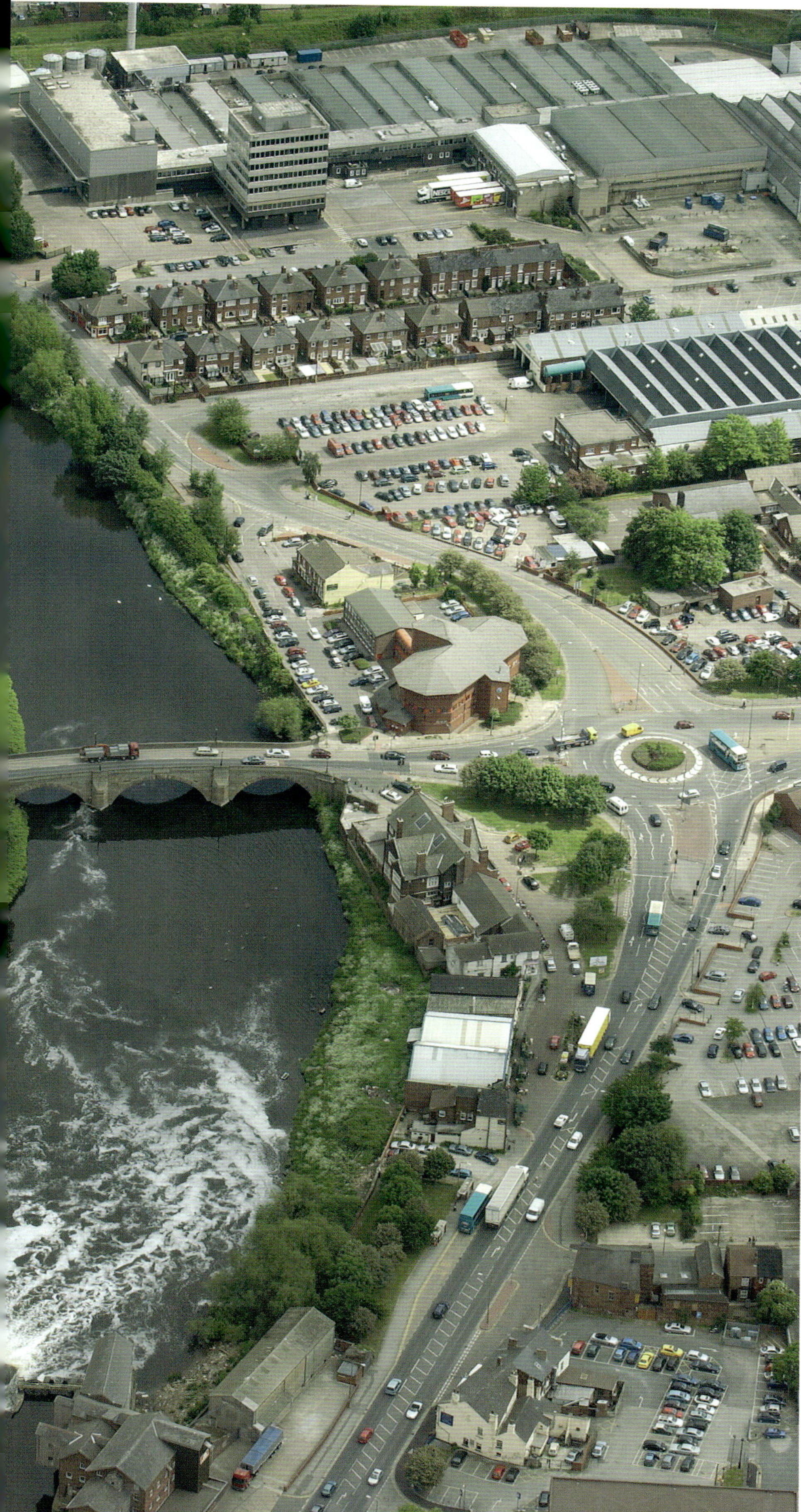

CASTLEFORD *(left & far left)*

The name Castleford is a corruption of Castreford, "the ford by the Roman fort". It was here, where the Roman military road Ermine Street crossed the river Aire, that the Roman station called *Legeolium* was located. The ford has now gone and the main river crossing is by means of a three-arch bridge built in the early 19th century. Castleford's growth was based on manufacturing and coalmining. The photograph on the far left is from the north-west over the town towards the M62 motorway which runs from left to right beyond the southern edge of the town. The site of Hickson's chemical works, the last chemical company in Castleford, can be seen in the foreground of the photograph on the far left.

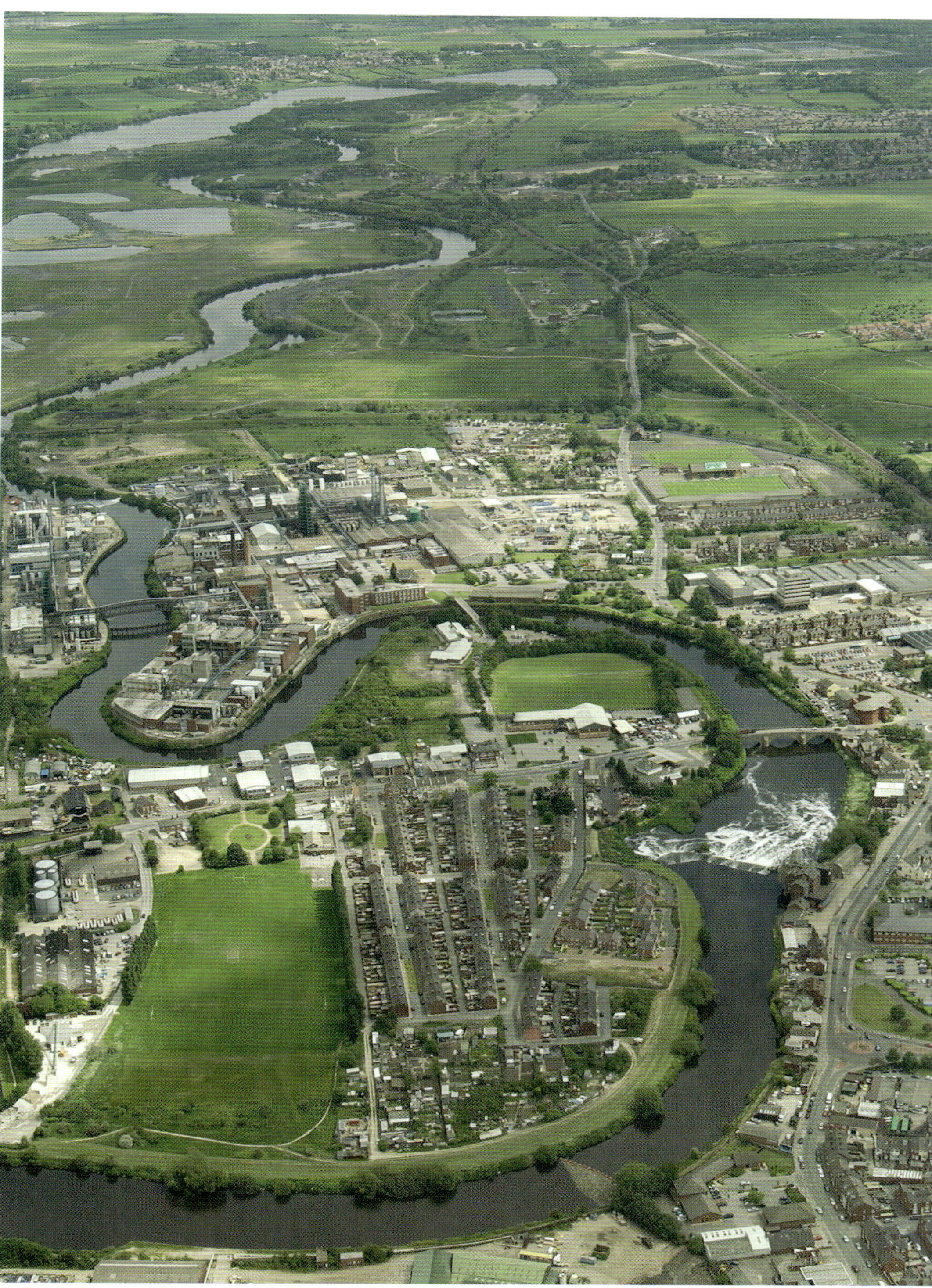

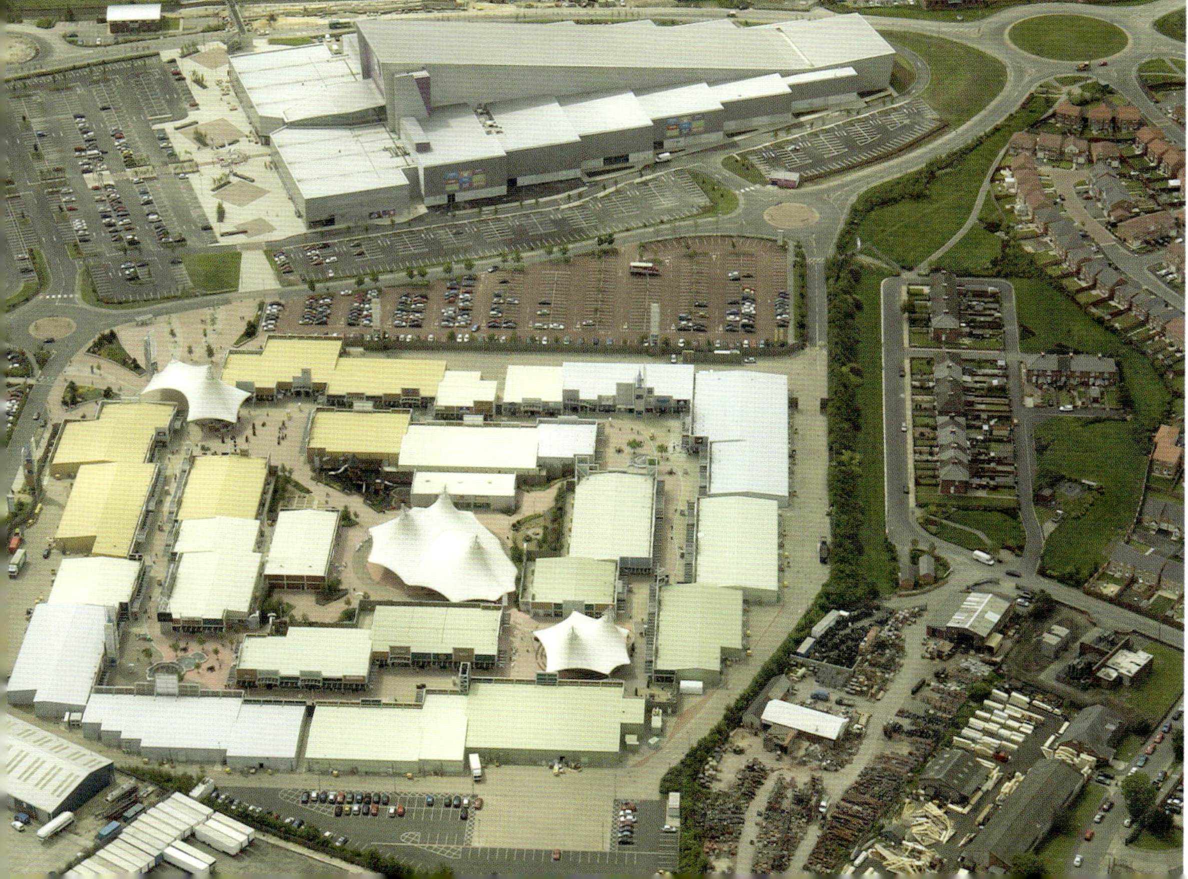

CASTLEFORD FROM THE WEST LOOKING TOWARDS FAIRBURN INGS *(above)*

This view of the town shows in the right middle ground Castleford Tigers rugby league club's ground, "the Jungle", on Wheldon Road and in the background Fairburn Ings RSPB nature reserve. This reserve is the ideal place to watch wetland birds. In summer redshank, snipe and lapwings breed and in winter there are thousands of ducks and geese. Many wading birds also visit the reserve on their autumn and spring migrations.

JUNCTION 32 OUTLET SHOPPING VILLAGE

(left)

This retail park (formerly Freeport Castleford) is a modern addition to Castleford's townscape. Located in Glasshoughton between junction 32 of the M62 motorway and the centre of the town, it is a designer outlet village with more than 65 shops selling a wide range of merchandise, designer fashion, children's wear, books and music. There is also a large DIY warehouse, a hotel and parking for 1,000 cars. Next door, with its sloping roofline, is Castleford Xscape where under one roof can be found real snow slopes, ice climbing walls, bowling alleys, a multi-screen cinema and cafes and restaurants. At night it becomes a "dine and dance destination".

KNOTTINGLEY & FERRYBRIDGE *(below)*

This view sweeps westwards across Knottingley, on slightly raised ground beside the river Aire, to Ferrybridge and its eight power station cooling towers. Electricity production began at Ferrybridge in 1927 when it became one of a large number of small power stations located near to the mainly urban markets they served. Massive expansion to make Ferrybridge Britain's largest coal-fired power station took place in the 1960s. The waters of the nearby river Aire have from the beginning been used not only to transport coal to the station but also to supply the steam-powered turbines.

PONTEFRACT CASTLE *(right)*

This is all that remains of what must have been one of Yorkshire's most impressive medieval stone keep castles. What can be seen here are the remains of the inner bailey with its surviving wall, and the remains of a postern gate and a chapel. Originally built as a timber motte and bailey castle in the late 11th century by its Norman lord Ilbert de Lacy, it was "slighted" (levelled with the ground) in 1649 following the end of the Civil War. The space was reputedly used for a time as a field for growing liquorice for making the famous Pontefract cakes. It is now a recreation ground.

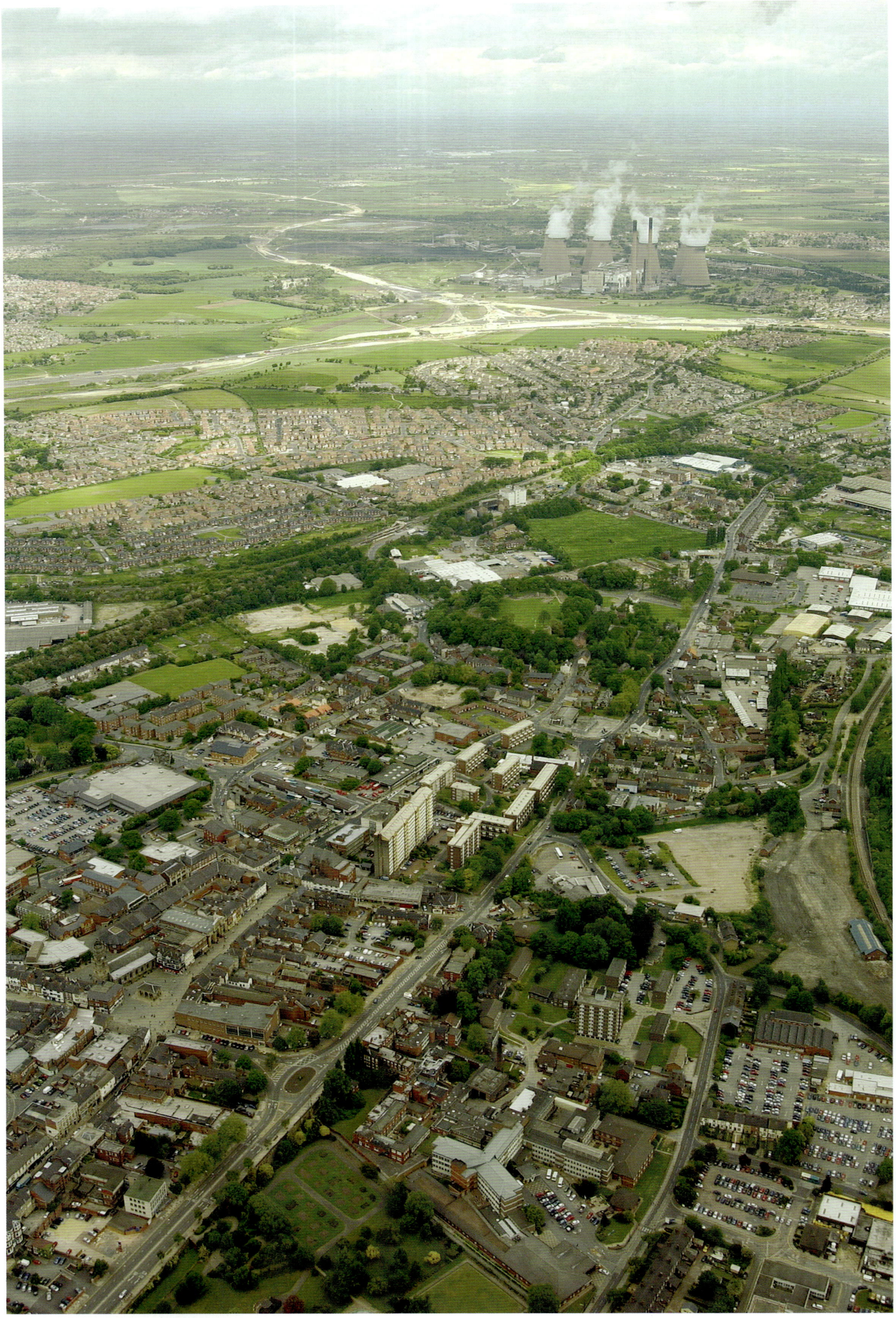

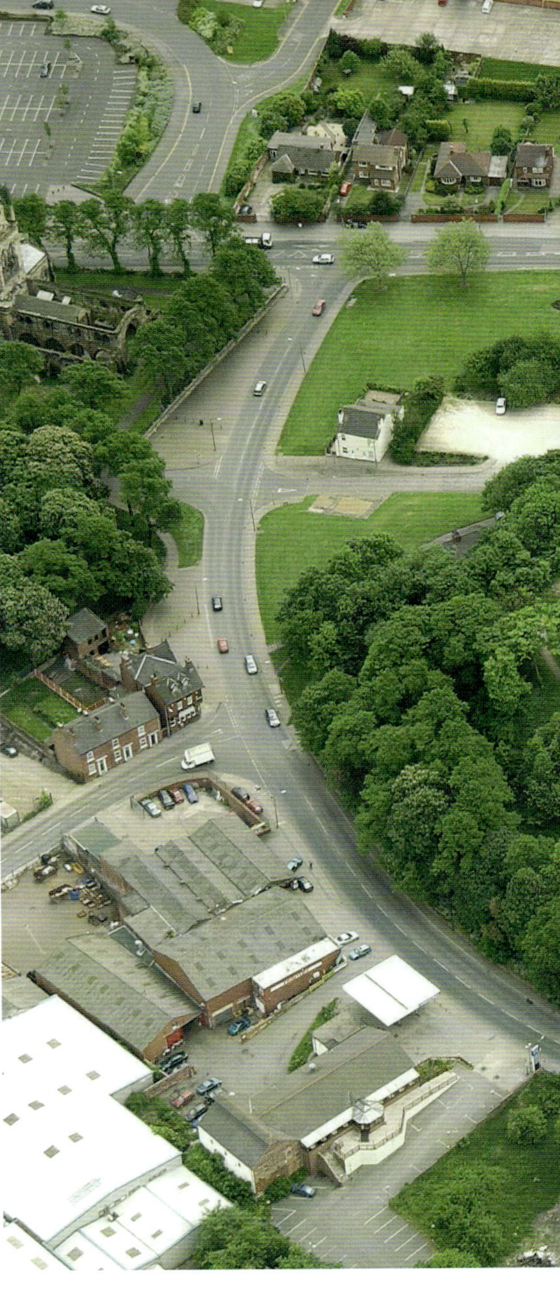

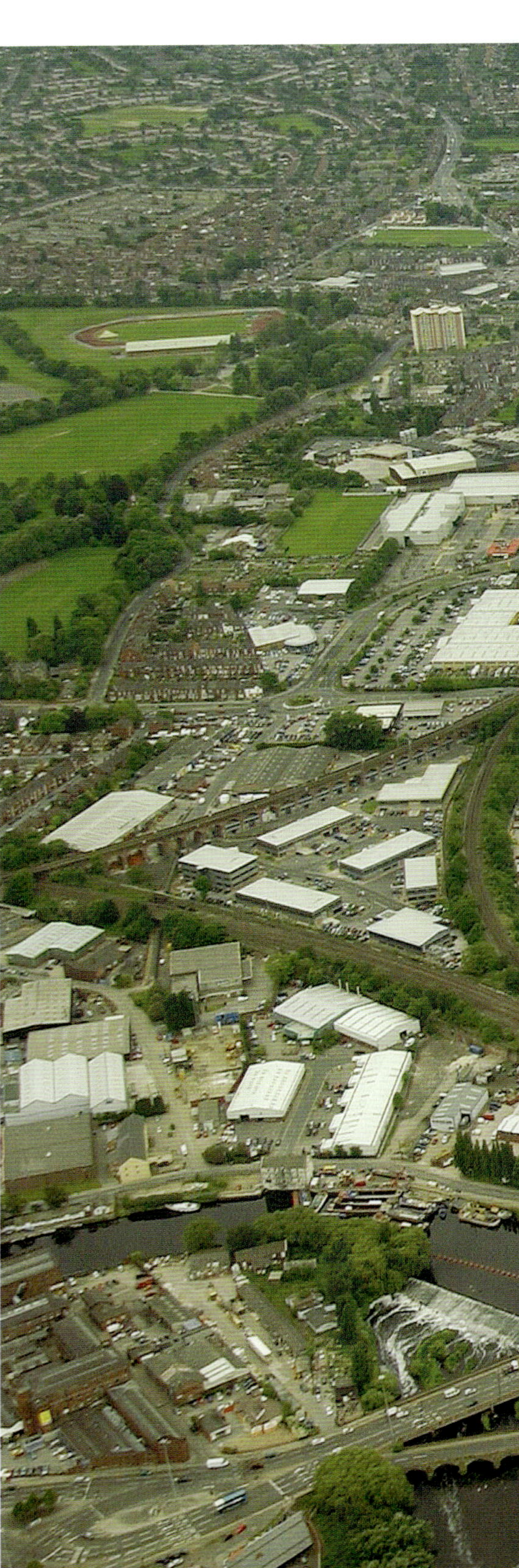

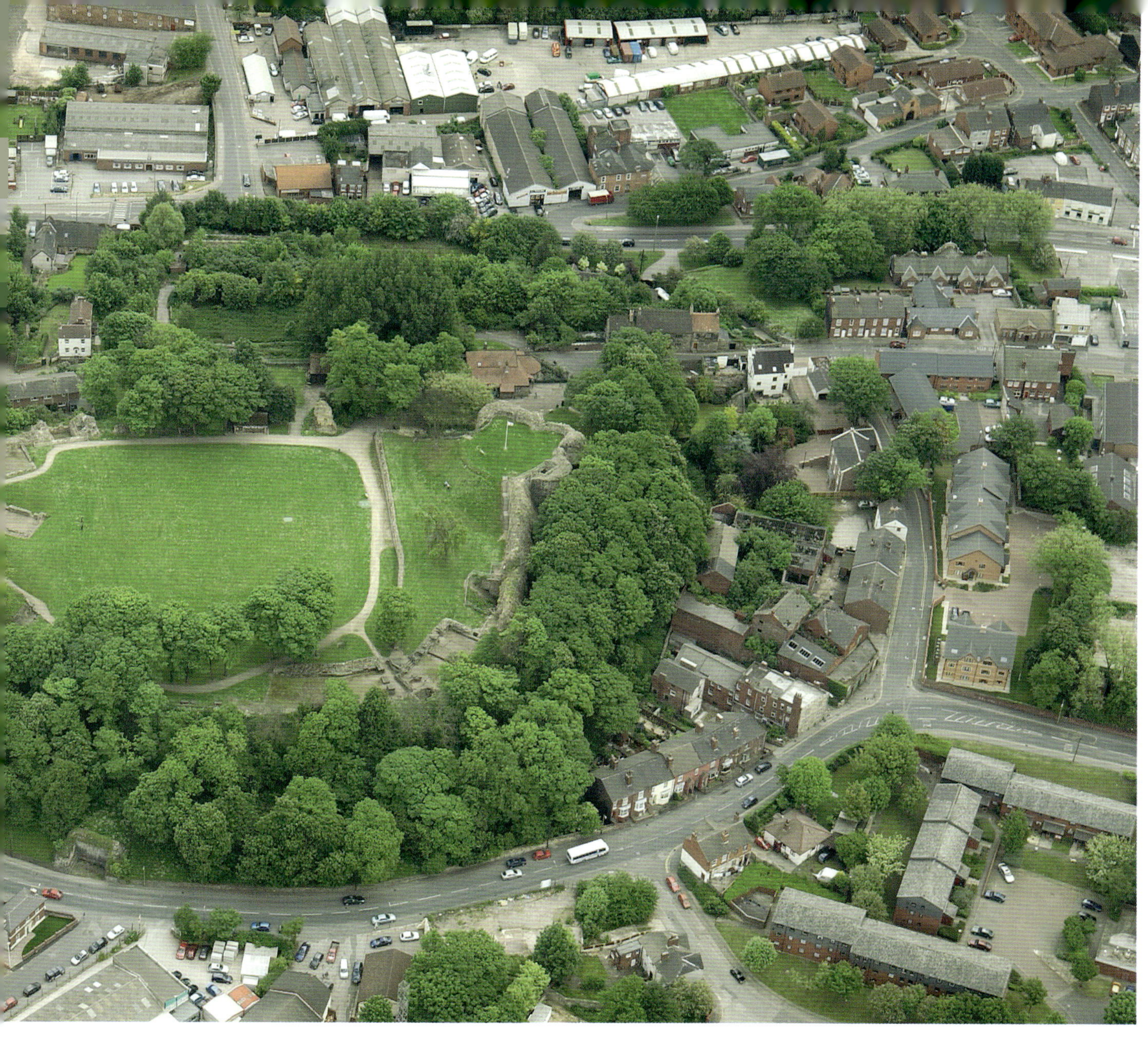

WAKEFIELD *(below)*

This panoramic view of Wakefield looks in a north-westerly direction over the urban area towards Wrenthorpe. In the medieval and early modern period Wakefield was an important market town and was the centre of the Yorkshire clothing trade before the rise of Leeds and Bradford. In the 1720s Daniel Defoe described Wakefield as large, handsome and rich. Until 1974, and local government reorganisation, the town was the administrative capital for the West Riding County Council. Its early importance is reflected in two important medieval buildings that survive. In the foreground can be seen the medieval chapel built about 1350 on the bridge over the river Calder, one of only four surviving bridge chapels in the whole country. The other fine medieval building is the Perpendicular-style cathedral, until 1888 the parish church of All Saints, standing on Kirkgate (Church Street) in the centre of the town. Sir Nikolaus Pevsner commented that Wakefield had what few towns in England could boast – a skyline. The highest feature in Wakefield's skyline is the cathedral spire, 247ft (75m) high. Two other important features of Wakefield's skyline stand in Wood Street, the tower of the Town Hall rising to 190ft (58m) and the domed tower of the former West Riding County Hall rising to 130ft (40m).

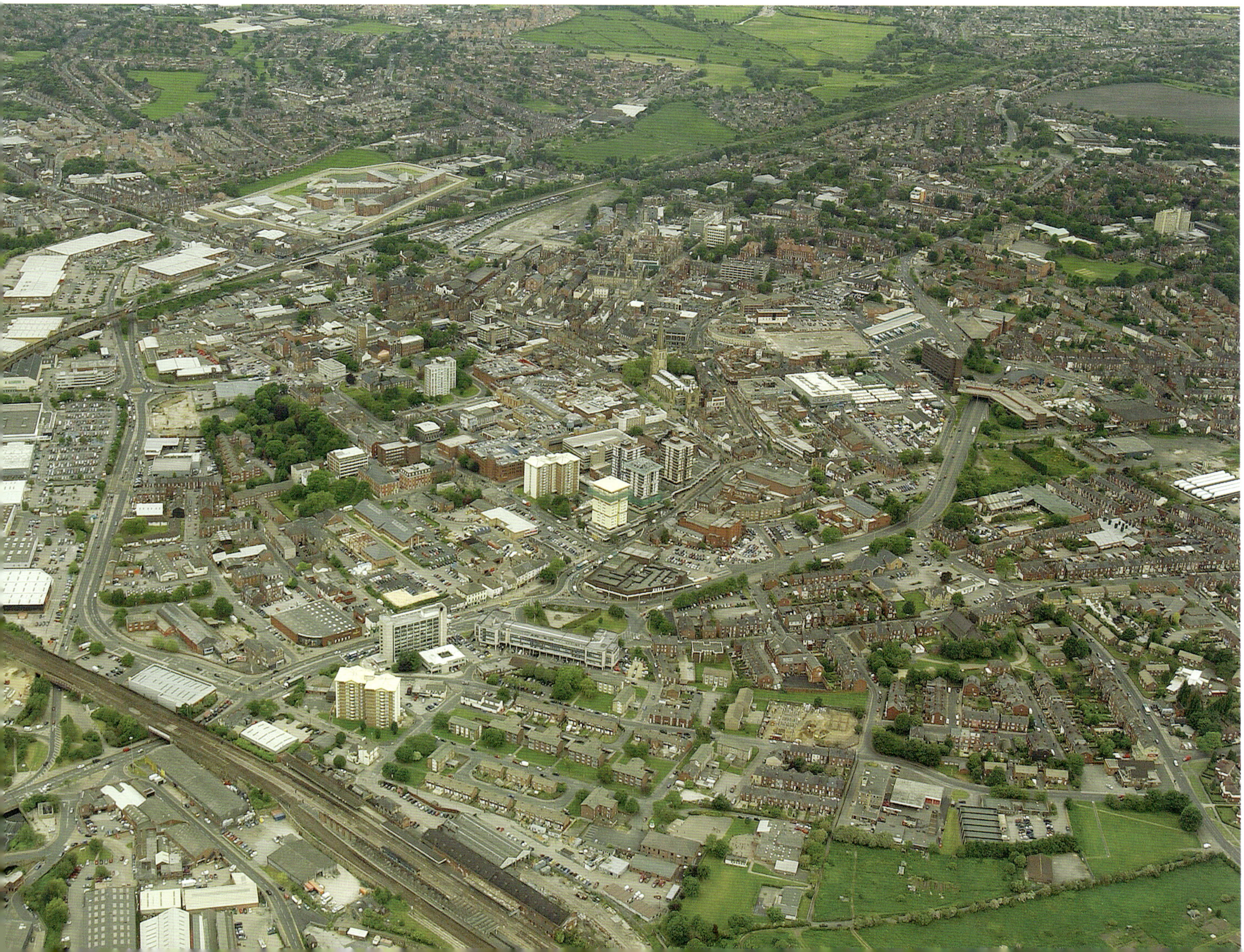

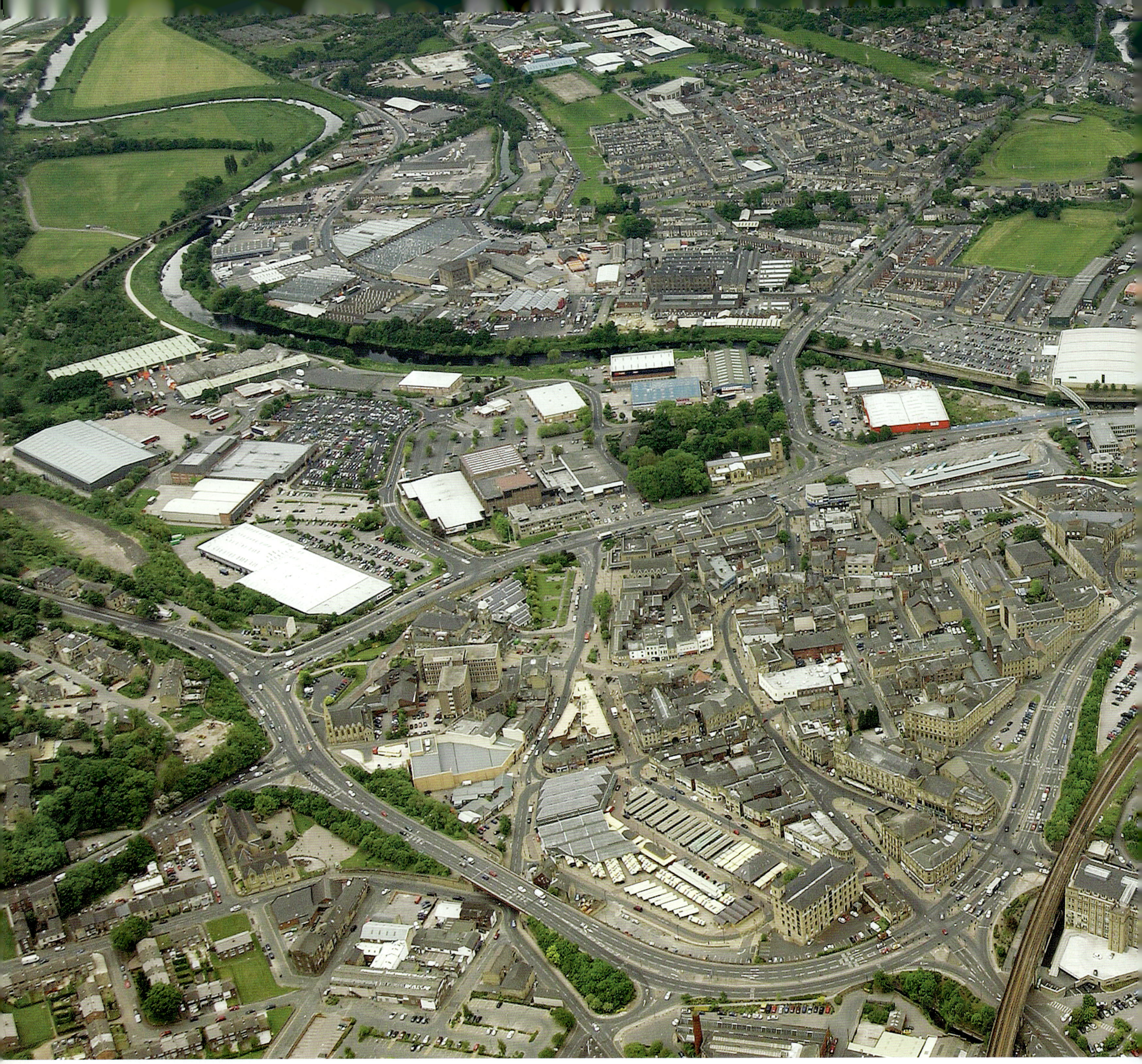

DEWSBURY *(above)*

This panoramic view of Dewsbury shows the town from the north with the town centre lying outside a great meander on the river Calder. The river is bridged in three places, with the principal road (Wilson Street leading to Saville Road, the B6409) linking the town centre with extensive industrial, warehousing and residential development in Saville Town which occupies the level ground within the meander itself. In the foreground most of Dewsbury's town centre is hemmed in by the modern road system of Dewsbury Ring Road and the railway line between Leeds and Huddersfield. The town street names such as Market Street and Old Westgate betray its medieval origins while Nelson Street and Wellington Street reflect its 19th-century expansion. Some of the most striking buildings in and around the town centre are 19th-century multi-storey textile mills and wool warehouses that stand out in stark contrast with the modern flat-roofed one-storey warehouses, workshops and stores. Also well in evidence are the stalls of Dewsbury's outdoor market.

LEEDS-BRADFORD AIRPORT *(right)*

Originally known as Yeadon Aerodrome, Leeds-Bradford International Airport is on the former Yeadon Moor, six miles north-east of Bradford and six miles north-west of Leeds. The first club flight from the aerodrome took place in 1931 and scheduled flights began four years later in 1935 to Blackpool and the Isle of Man, Newcastle and Edinburgh. RAF 609 squadron was formed at Yeadon in 1936 and civil flights stopped in 1939 with the outbreak of the Second World War but resumed again in 1947. During the war military aircraft at the nearby Avro works received their first test flights at Yeadon. By 1955 international flights to Ostend and Dusseldorf had been added to the domestic destinations. Scheduled flights to London began in 1960 and in 1978 the first flight for holidaymakers to Spain took place. The terminal building was destroyed by fire in 1965 but was rebuilt and re-opened in 1968 and significant extensions and improvements have been made since then. Two million passengers flew from the airport in 2003.

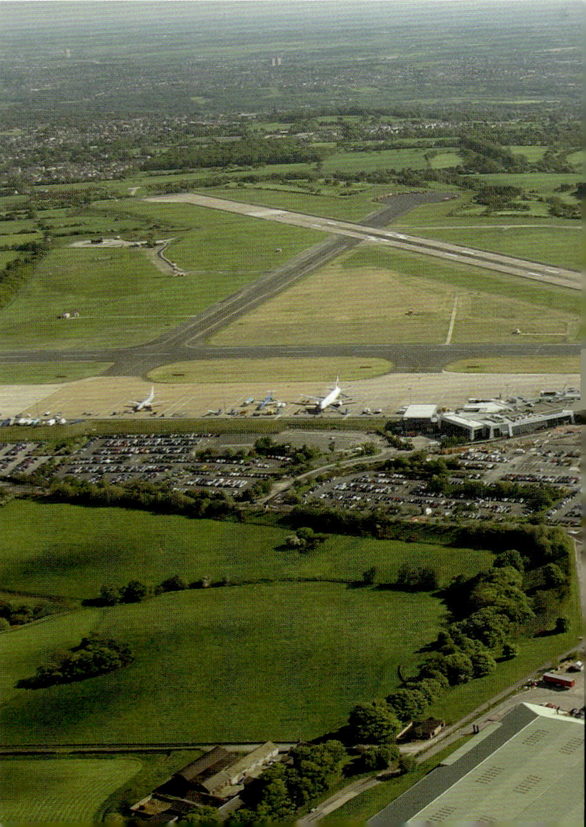

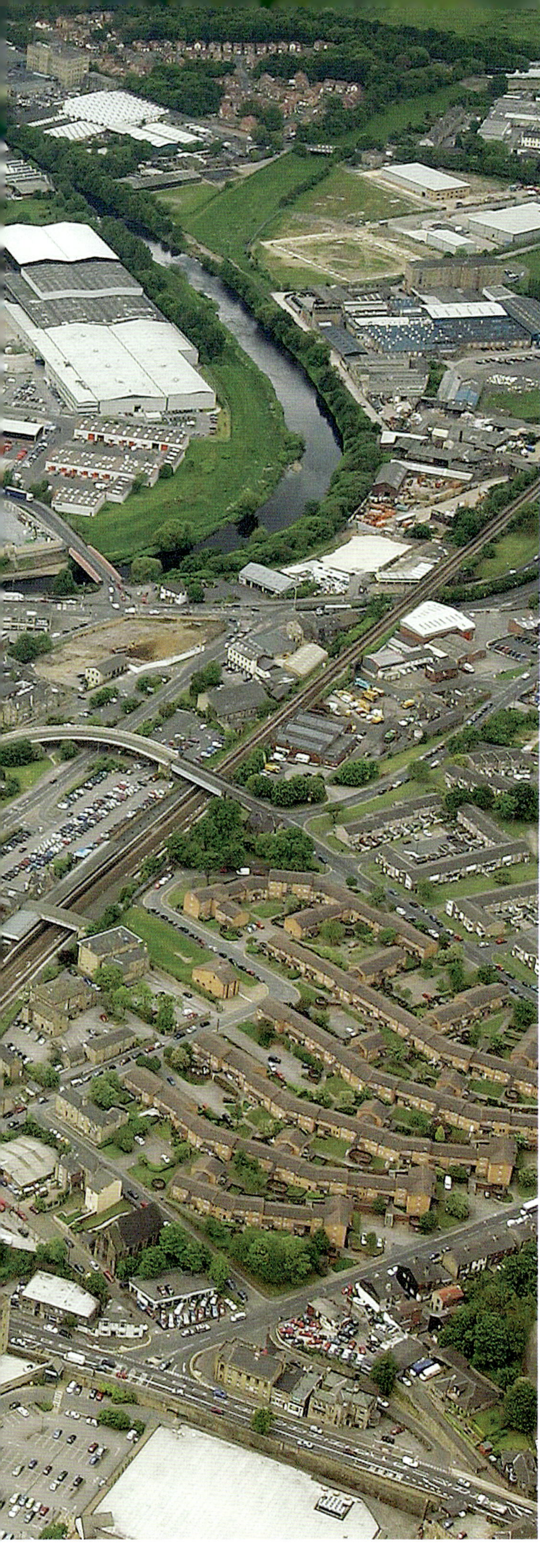

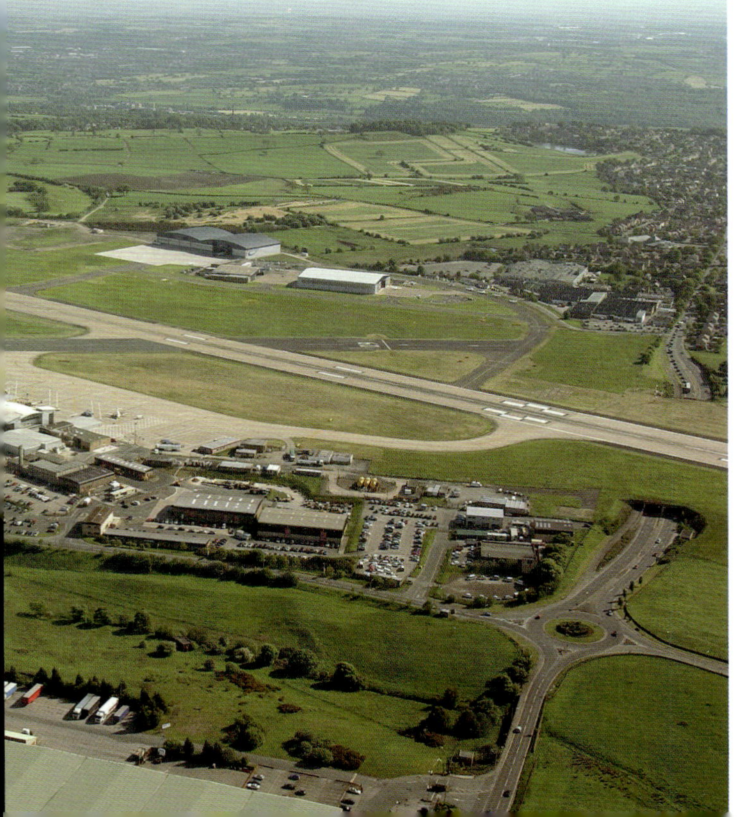

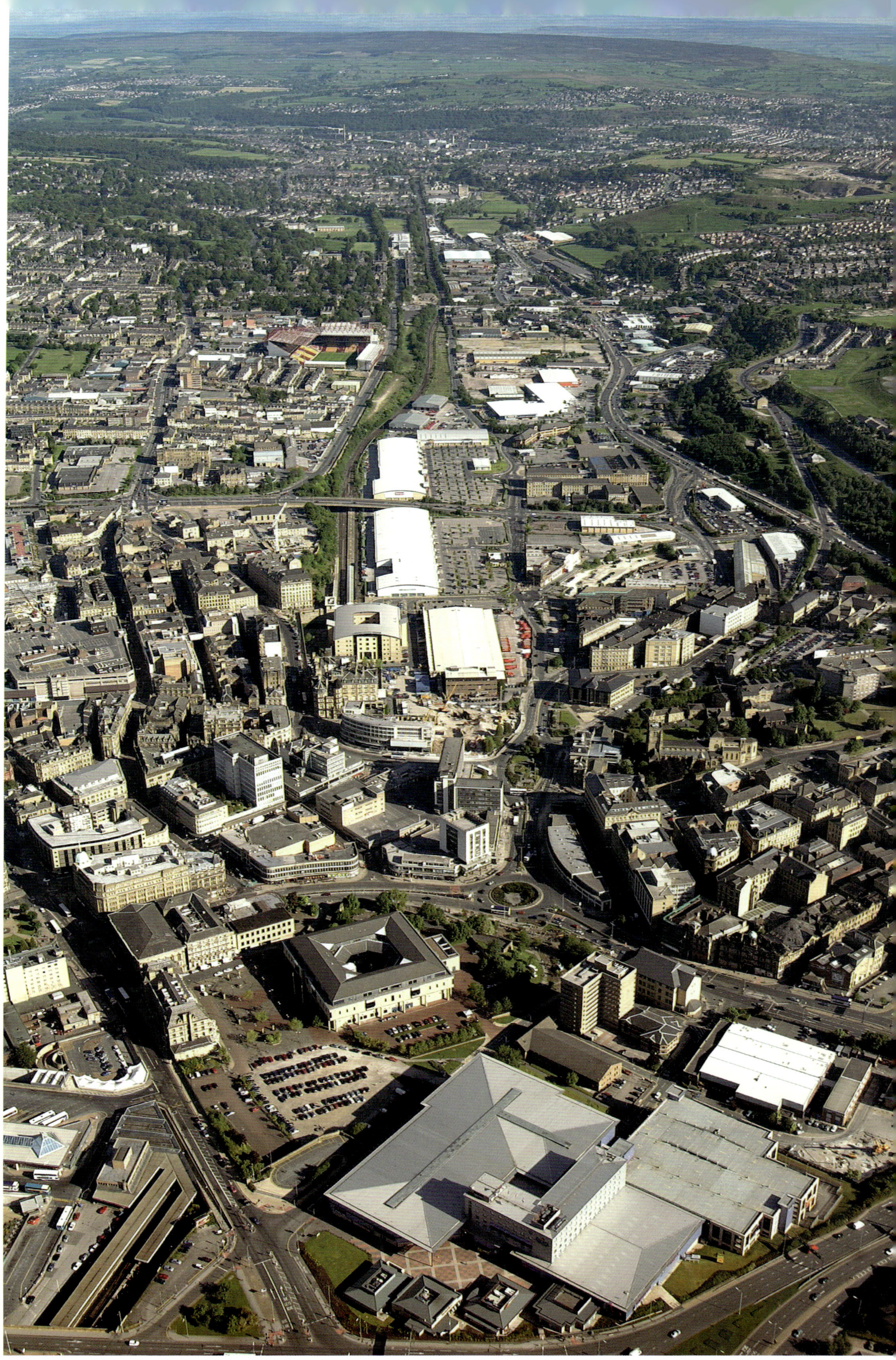

BRADFORD *(above)*

The cloth trade had made Bradford a wealthy town by the late Middle Ages and this prosperity continued through the Tudor and Stuart periods. But its great period of expansion came in the 19th century when the population grew from about 13,000 in 1801 to 280,000 a century later. The Bradford branch of the Leeds and Liverpool Canal opened in 1774, the railway that came in 1846, and local collieries that produced the fuel for the textile mills were key factors in this period of sustained industrial expansion. Popularly known as "Worstedopolis", Bradford was the world centre in the Victorian period for the production of worsted, made from long wools.

This view of Bradford today is from the south-east looking over the city centre with the railway terminating at Forster Square Railway Station just to the south of the flyover carrying the A6181 (Hamm Strasse) beside the Forster Square Retail Park. Along the line of the railway can be seen Valley Parade football stadium and beyond that the outer suburbs of the city and on to Shipley and Baildon with Rombalds Moor rising in the background.

Now fighting not to be dwarfed by modern development, Bradford Cathedral stands on a slight rise on the eastern (right) side of Forster Square. This was St Peter's parish church until raised to cathedral status in 1919. Made of millstone grit it has a fine Perpendicular western tower constructed between 1493 and 1508. In the immediate foreground can be seen The Leisure Exchange, 205,000sq ft (19,000sq m) of space, the tenth largest leisure scheme in the UK.

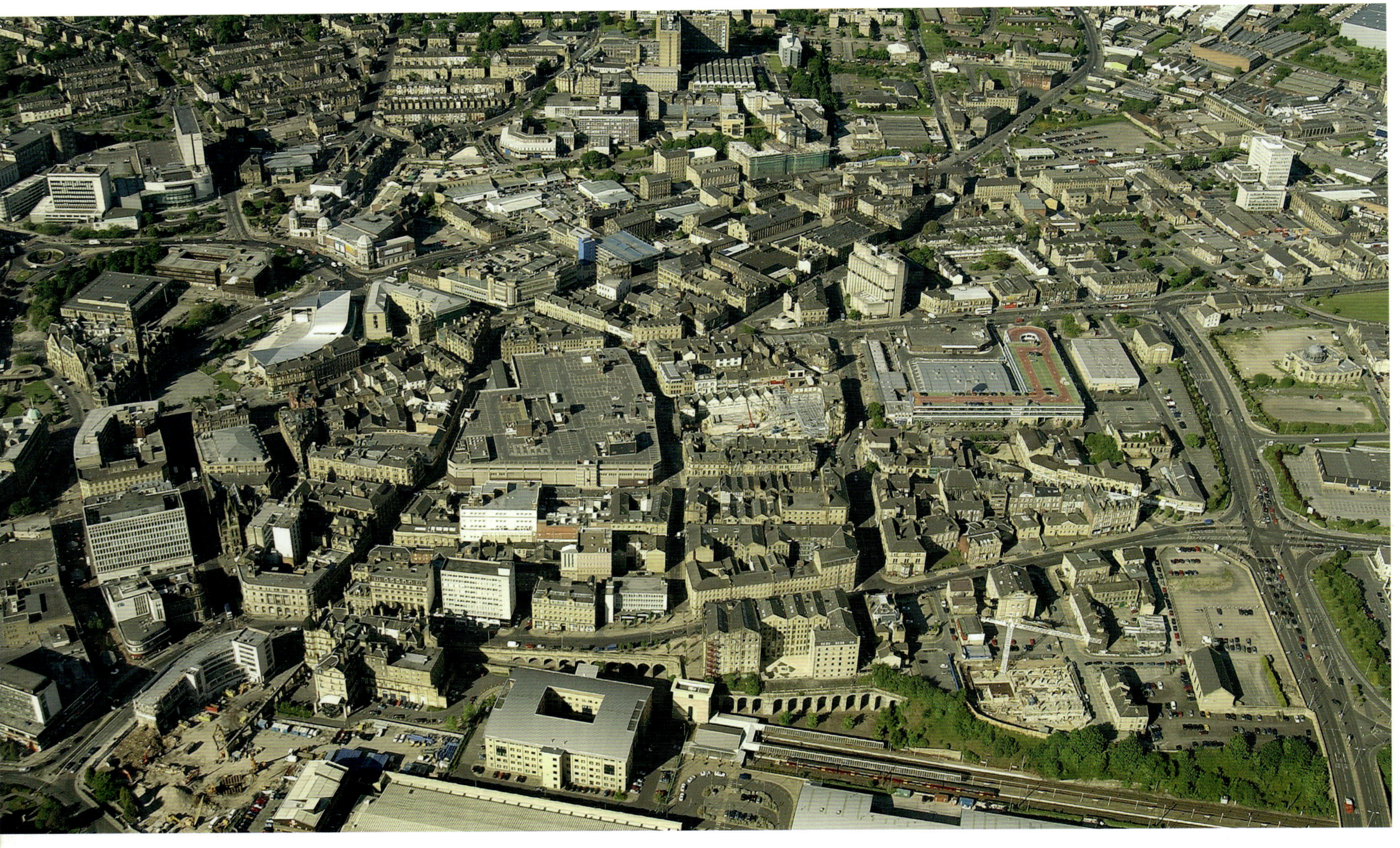

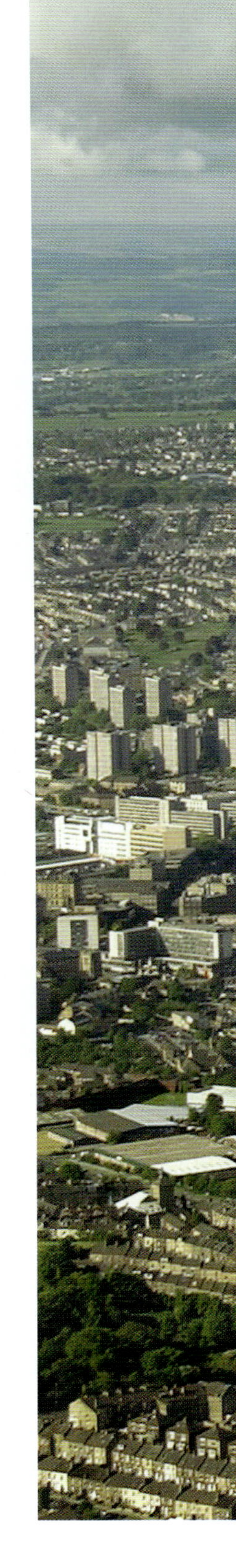

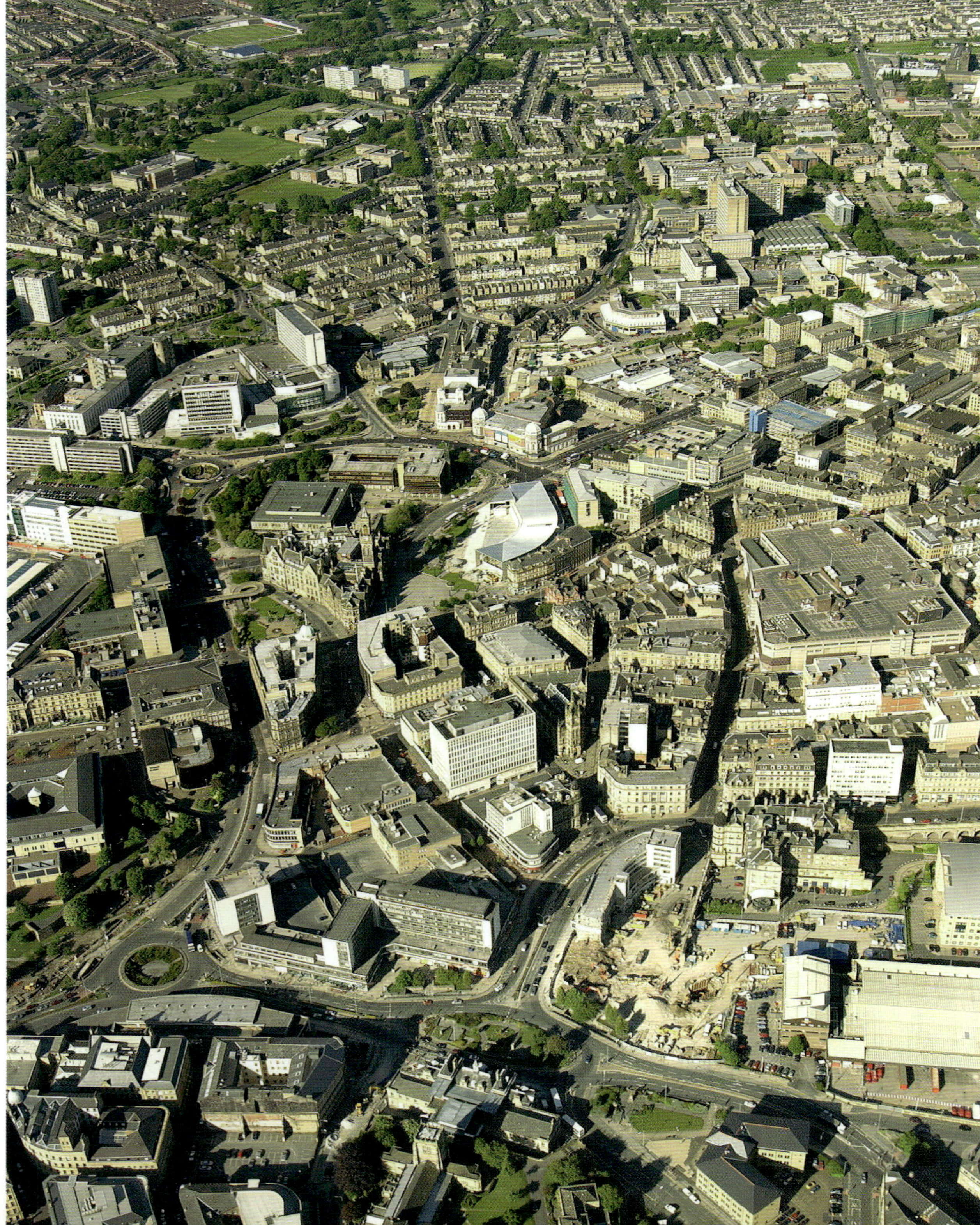

THREE VIEWS OF CENTRAL BRADFORD

(above, left and above right)

All three photographs show various parts of central Bradford from the east. In the foreground of the photograph above can be seen the railway terminus at Forster Square. Running away on the right-hand side of the photograph is the A6181 (Hamm Strasse) with the junction with Manningham Lane, Manor Row and Cheapside and further away the junction with Westgate/Godwin Street, all clearly visible. Between the railway and Westgate/Godwin Street can be seen the roofs of Rawson Market, John Street Market, and the Arndale Centre and Kirkgate Market.

The photograph above right shows the same part of Bradford in the left middle ground but also taking in a wider view of the suburbs to the north and west of the city centre (including Thornton where the Brontë family lived before moving to Haworth) and beyond to the peripheral villages of Denholme and Oxenhope on the edge of the Pennine moors.

The photograph on the left shows a view of central Bradford looking along Hall Ings and Kirkgate to Godwin Street and beyond along Thornton Road. In the immediate foreground is a small part of that district of Bradford called "Little Germany" where 19th-century German wool merchants built their spectacular warehouses in Greek revival, Italianate and Gothic styles (seen more clearly in the photograph on the previous page). Also visible are the law courts and the roof of the Arndale Centre and Kirkgate Market.

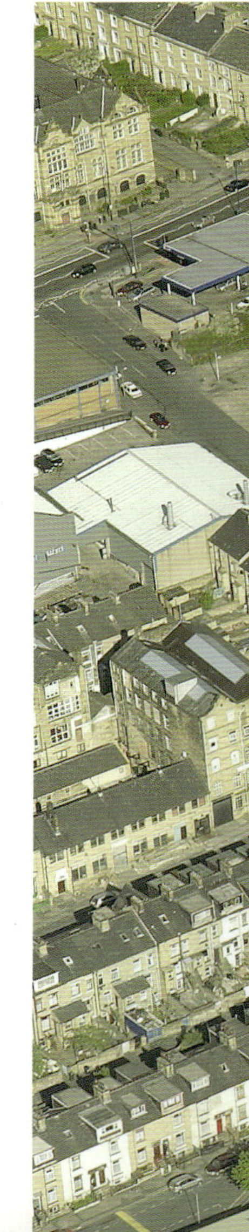

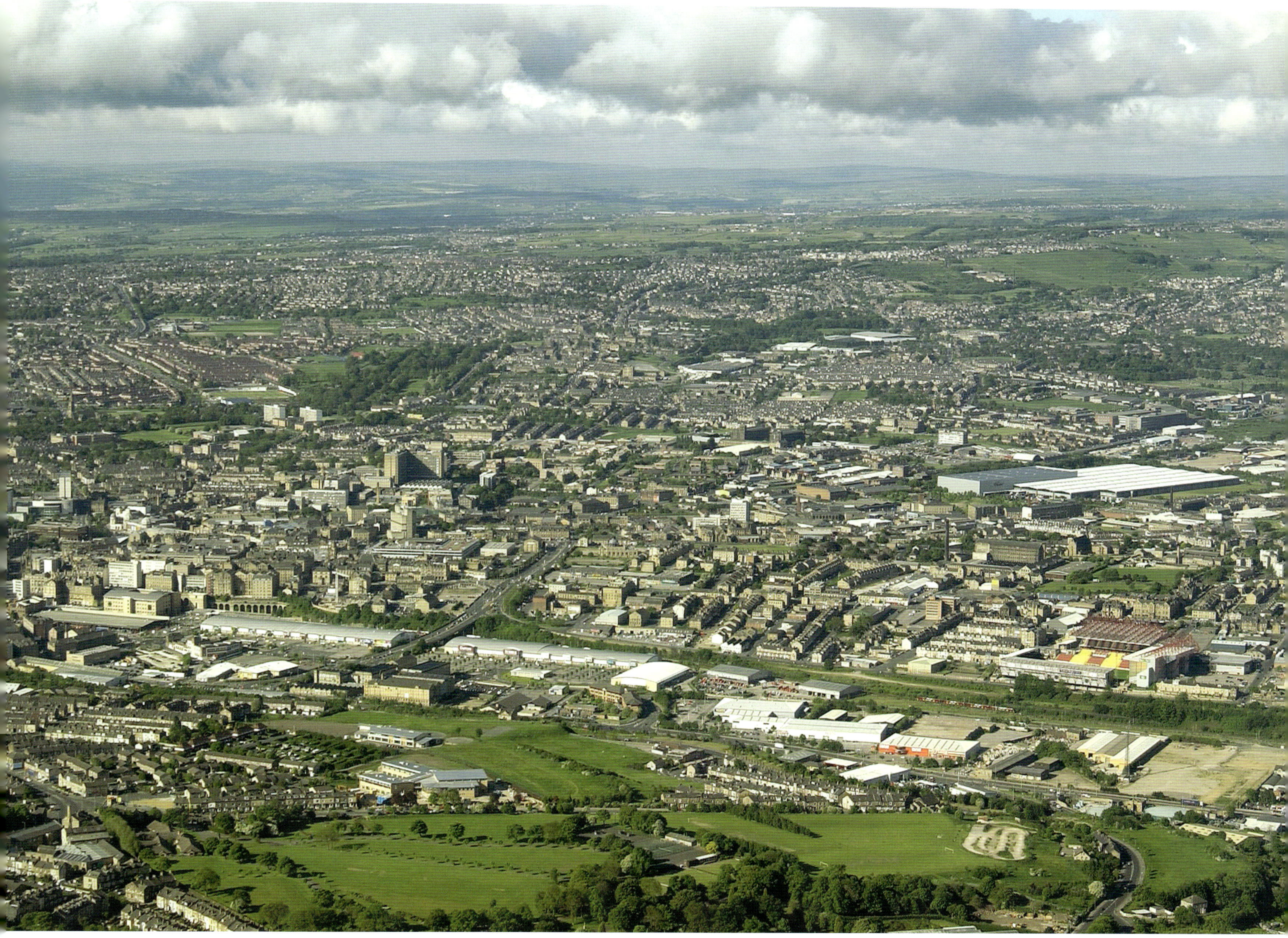

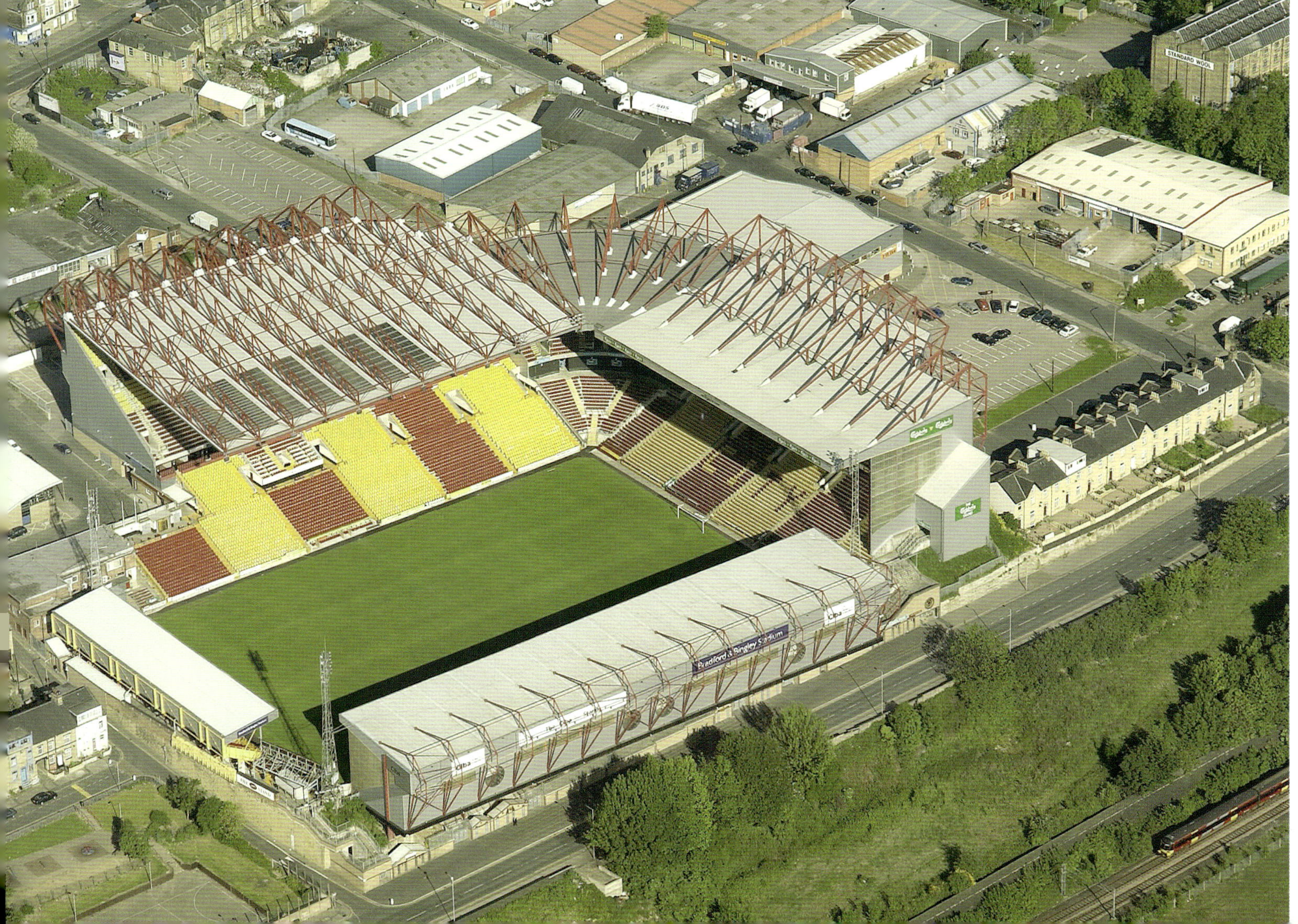

VALLEY PARADE *(left)*

Valley Parade is the home of Bradford City football club founded in 1903. The team colours, reflected in the colours of the stand seating, are claret and amber. They were FA Cup winners in 1911, the first holders of the present trophy which coincidentally was made in Bradford. The record attendance at the ground was 39,146 at a cup tie against Burnley in March 1911. The modern ground capacity is 25,136. Disaster struck the club, the ground and the city on 11 May 1985 when a fire, thought to have been started by an accidentally discarded lighted match or cigarette end in a polystyrene cup in the old Main Stand, caused the death of 56 spectators and injured another 265. The subsequent enquiry led by Mr Justice Popplewell resulted in new legislation about safety regulations at the country's sports grounds. For a whole season the club played its home fixtures at neighbouring grounds before the new stadium was re-opened in May 1986 when the club team played (and beat) an England XI.

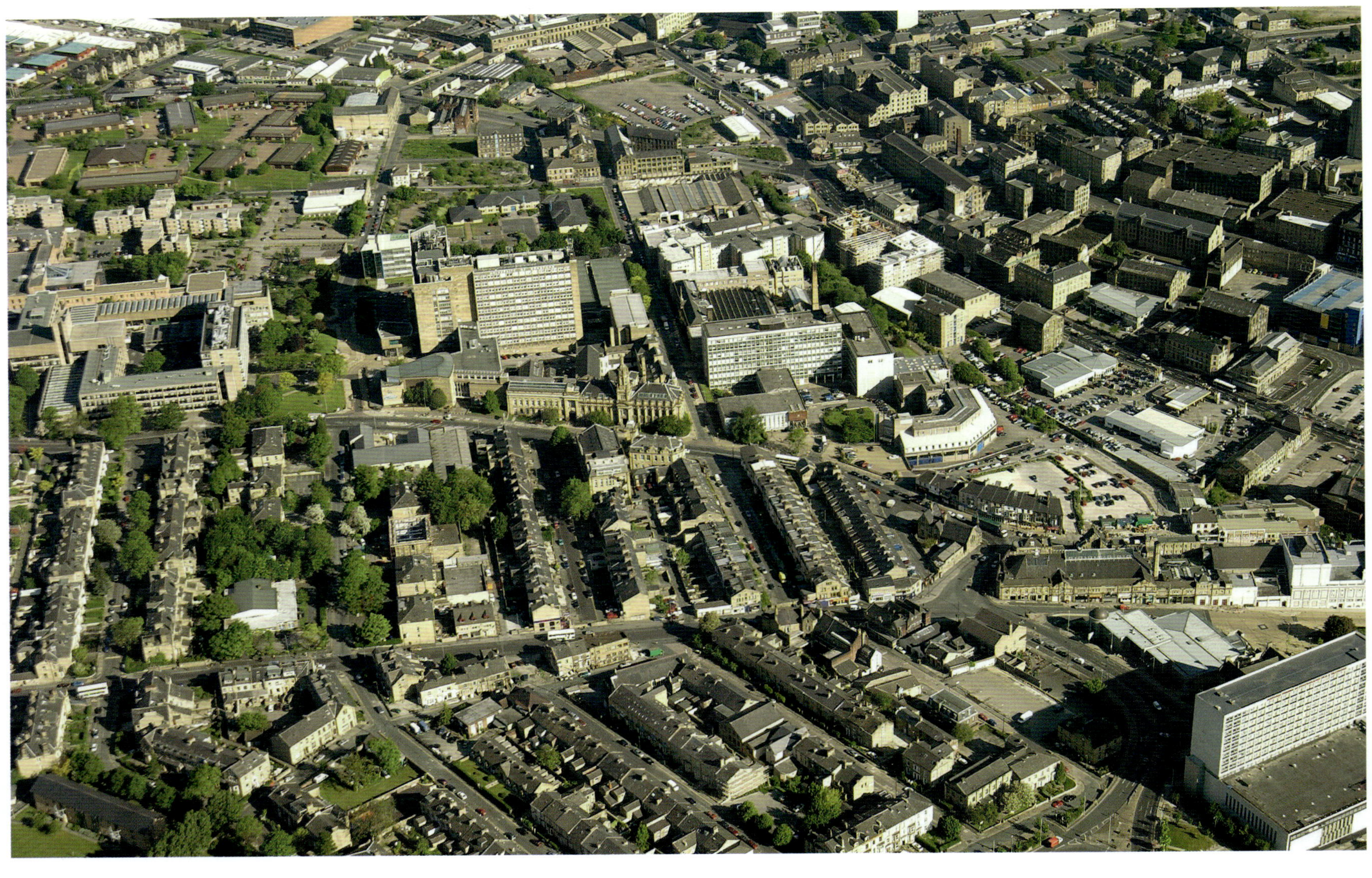

UNIVERSITY OF BRADFORD *(above)*

Bradford Institute of Technology received its Royal Charter to become the University of Bradford in 1966 and its first Chancellor was Prime Minister Harold Wilson. The university library is the JB Priestley Library, named after the Bradford-born novelist, dramatist and essayist. The university campus occupies a compact site just to the west of the city centre bounded by Listerhills Road in the north, Smith Street and Carlton Street in the east, Great Horton Road in the south and Shearbridge Road in the west. Millions of pounds continue to be invested on the campus to create a "21st Century Learning Village". Today Bradford is ranked number one among universities in the north of England for graduate employment.

MANNINGHAM MILLS *(below)*

Originally built in 1838, Manningham Mills (also known as Lister's Mill) were re-built in 1871-73 by local architects Andrews & Pepper for Samuel Cunliffe Lister following a fire. They became the largest silk-spinning and weaving mills in the country. The façade of the mills along Heaton Road is 350 yards (320m) long and the campanile chimney, which is based on one in the Piazza San Marco in Venice, is 249ft (76m) high and dominates the skyline. The imposing entrance has above it the Latin inscription *Fidem Parit Integritas* (Integrity produces confidence). A 19-week strike at the mill in 1890-91 played a major role in the formation of the Independent Labour Party. After years of dereliction the mills are being renovated and converted into stylish apartments.

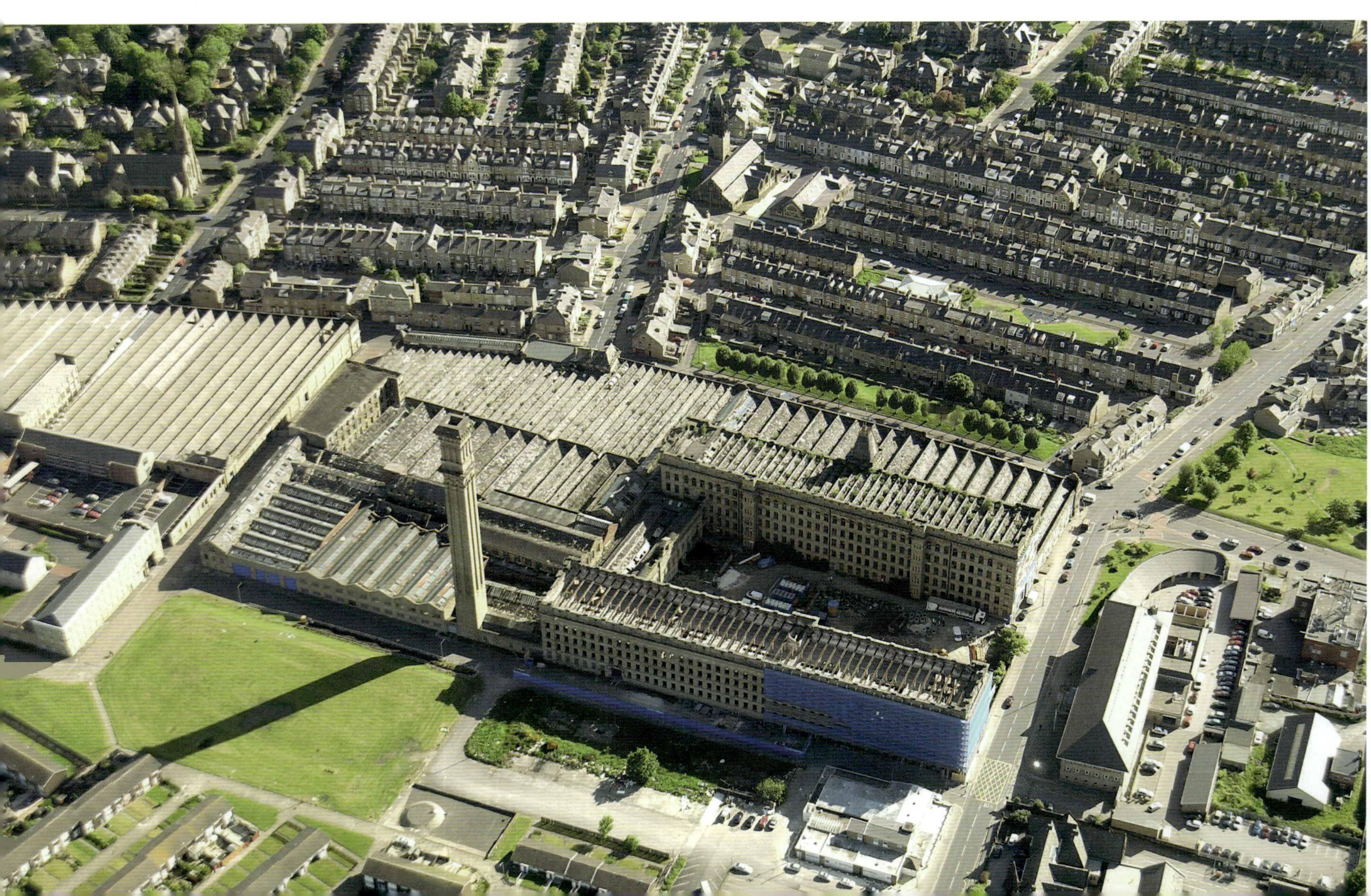

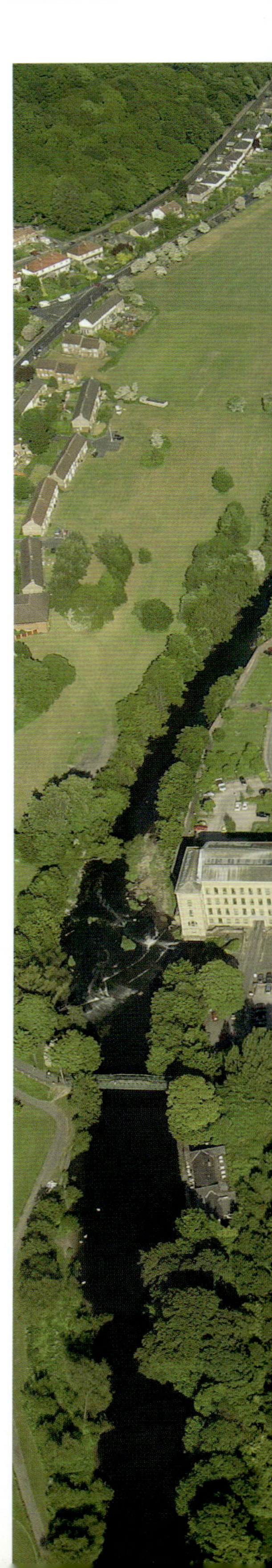

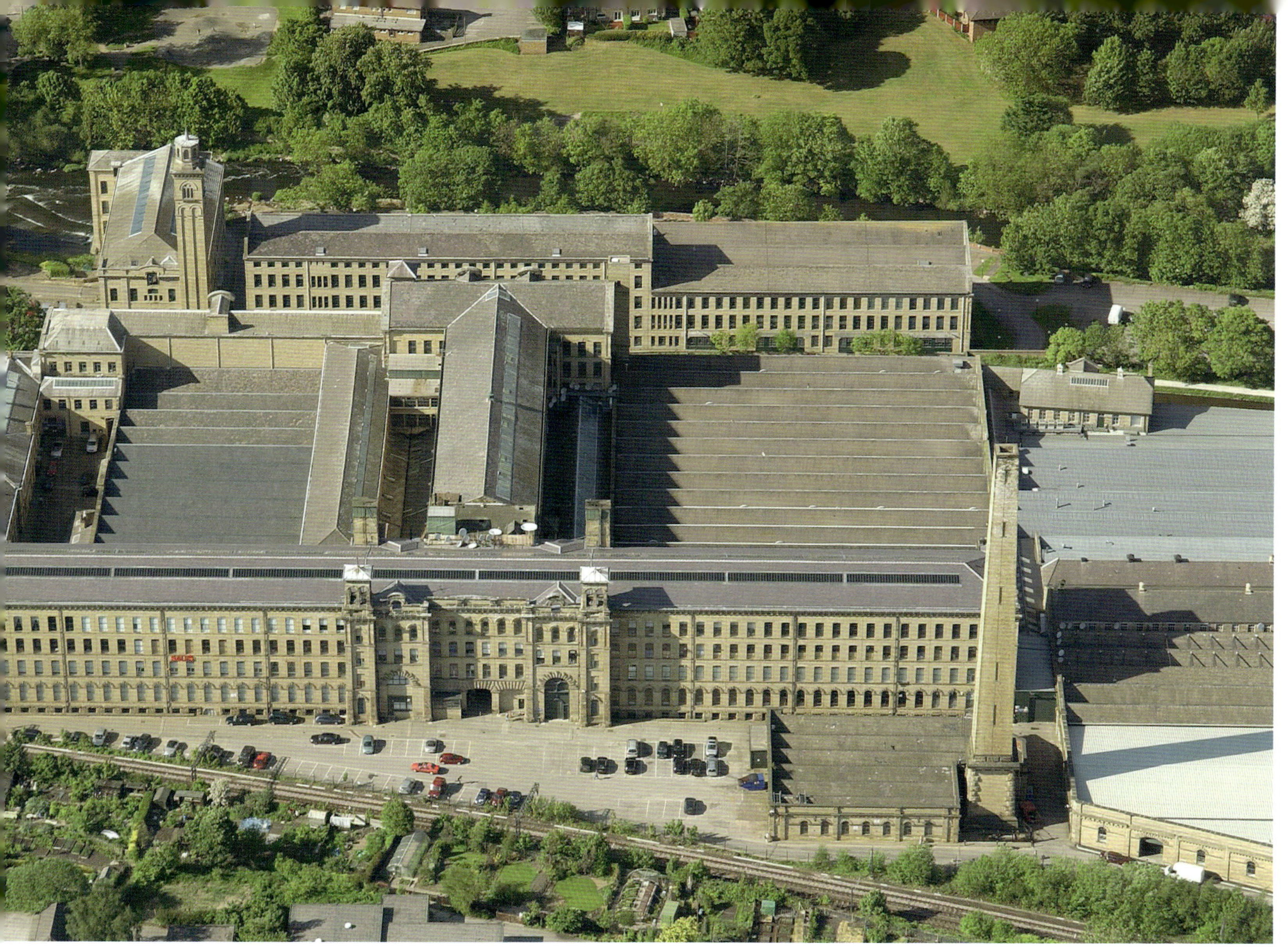

SALT'S MILL & SALTAIRE

(left, and below left & right)

Wealthy alpaca and mohair woollen cloth manufacturer, Sir Titus Salt, moved his mill and his workforce from Bradford to a more rural and healthy location to the north-west of the town in the Aire valley in the 1850s. He called his new industrial village Saltaire and the first large T-shaped six-storey mill to the south of the Leeds & Liverpool Canal was completed in 1853. Another mill, the New Mill, was completed in 1868, separated from the first mill by the canal. Both are in the Italianate style and have very tall campanile chimneys. Beside his mills Salt arranged for housing, places of worship and a school but there were no public houses. Altogether he built 895 houses laid out on a grid-iron street pattern some of which can be seen in the bottom left photograph. His architects also designed and built a beautiful congregational church which can be seen in both photographs below. Saltaire has been declared a World Heritage Site.

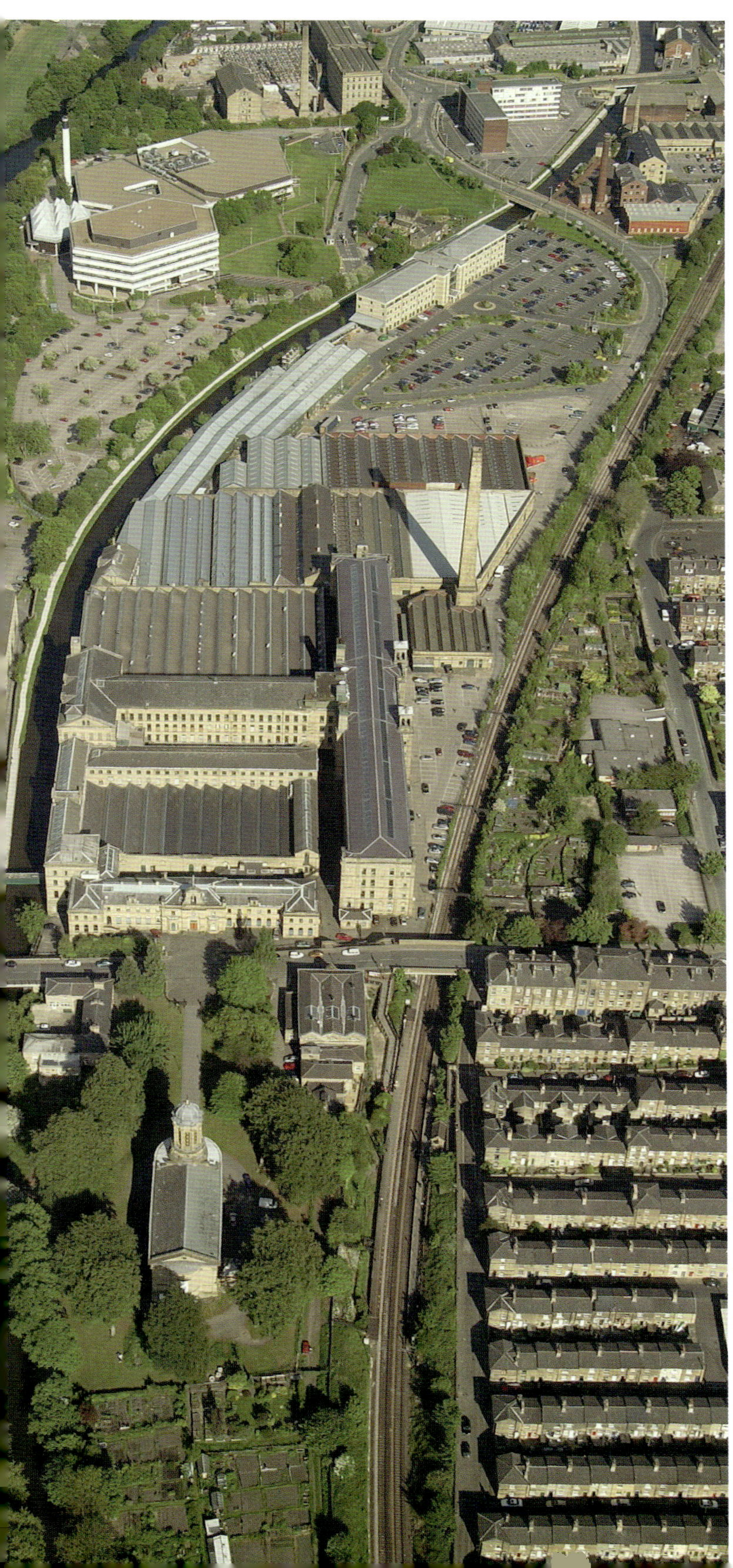

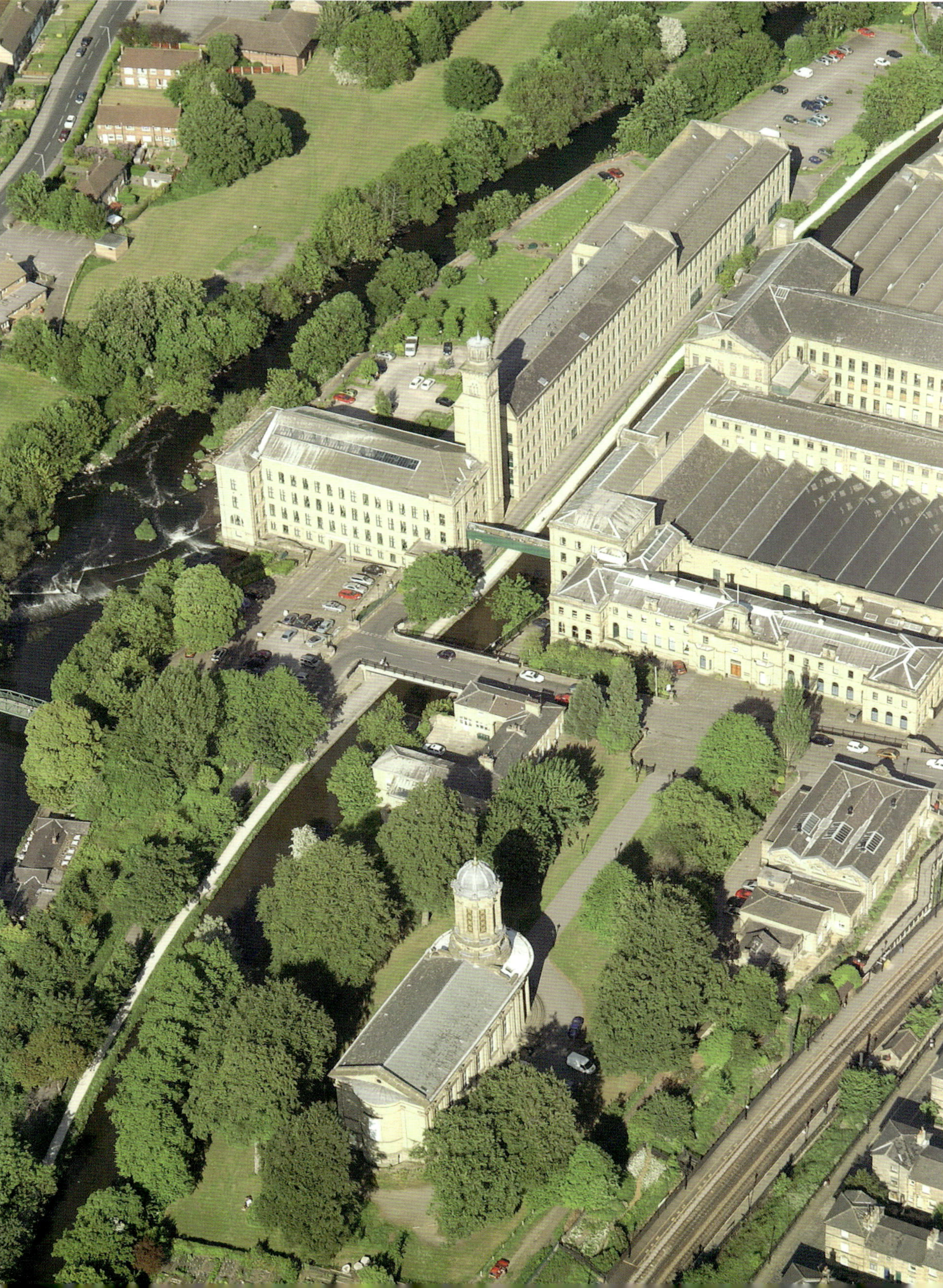

HAWORTH *(below & right)*

The photograph below shows Haworth from the north and the one on the right shows the village from the east. The steep main street of the village is still cobbled and contains antique shops, antiquarian bookshops and an old-fashioned apothecary shop. There is a network of footpaths from the village into the surrounding countryside. Visitors still flock to the Parsonage Museum, once the home of the Brontë family, where the three famous sisters, Emily, Charlotte and Anne wrote their well-loved novels: most famously Emily's *Jane Eyre*, Charlotte's *Wuthering Heights* and Anne's *The Tenant of Wildfell Hall*. The Brontë daughters were the children of the Revd Patrick Brontë who took his family to Haworth from Thornton near Bradford in 1820. Their mother died of cancer in 1821 and they were brought up by their aunt and mostly educated at home.

The most romantic approach to Haworth is by steam train on the Keighley & Worth Valley Railway (which can be seen in both photographs), lovingly portrayed in the 1970 film *The Railway Children*. This railway line was opened in 1867 by local mill-owners, but was closed by British Railways in 1962. It re-opened in 1968 and has been operated ever since by volunteers from the Keighley & Worth Valley Preservation Society.

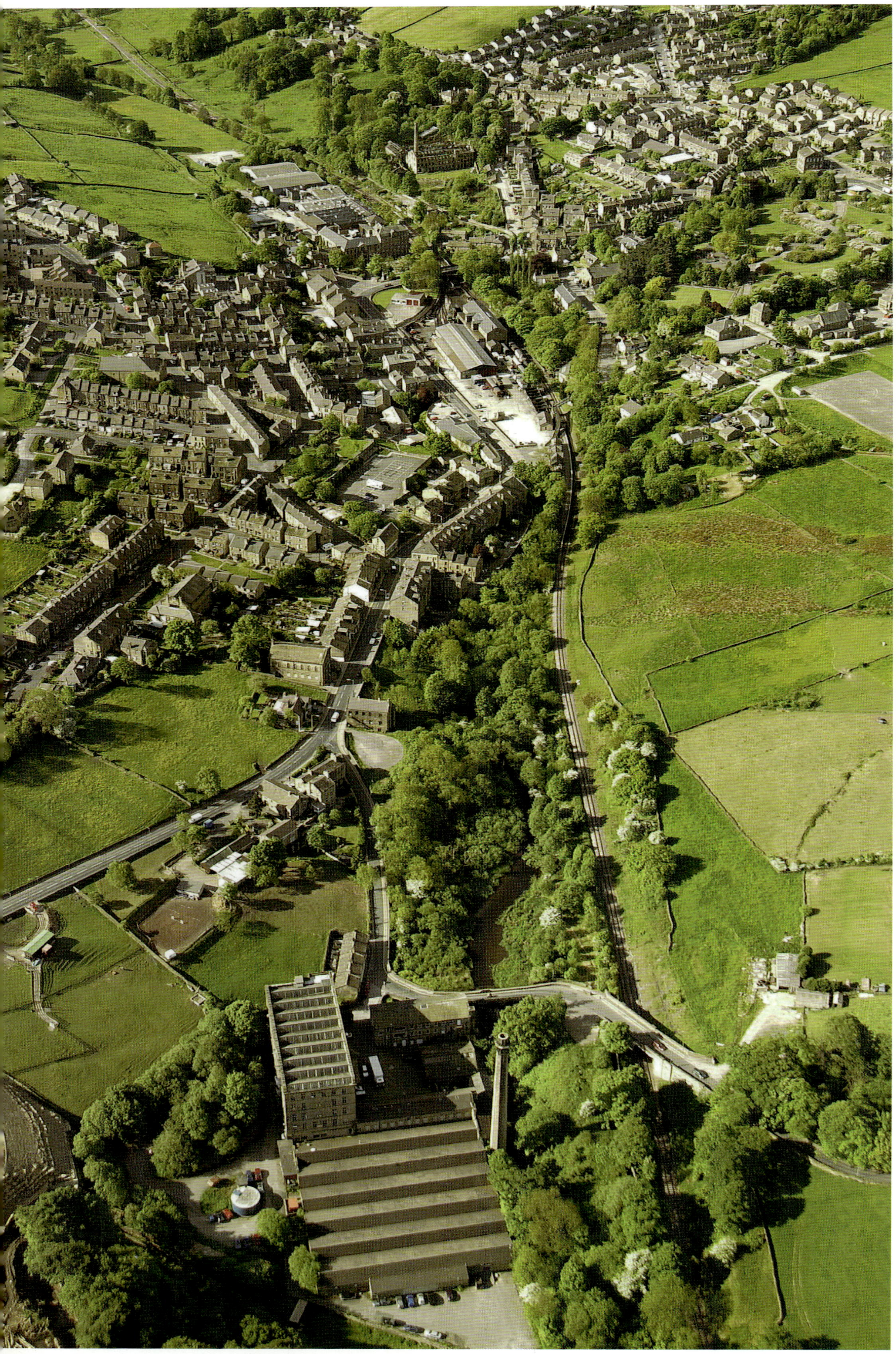

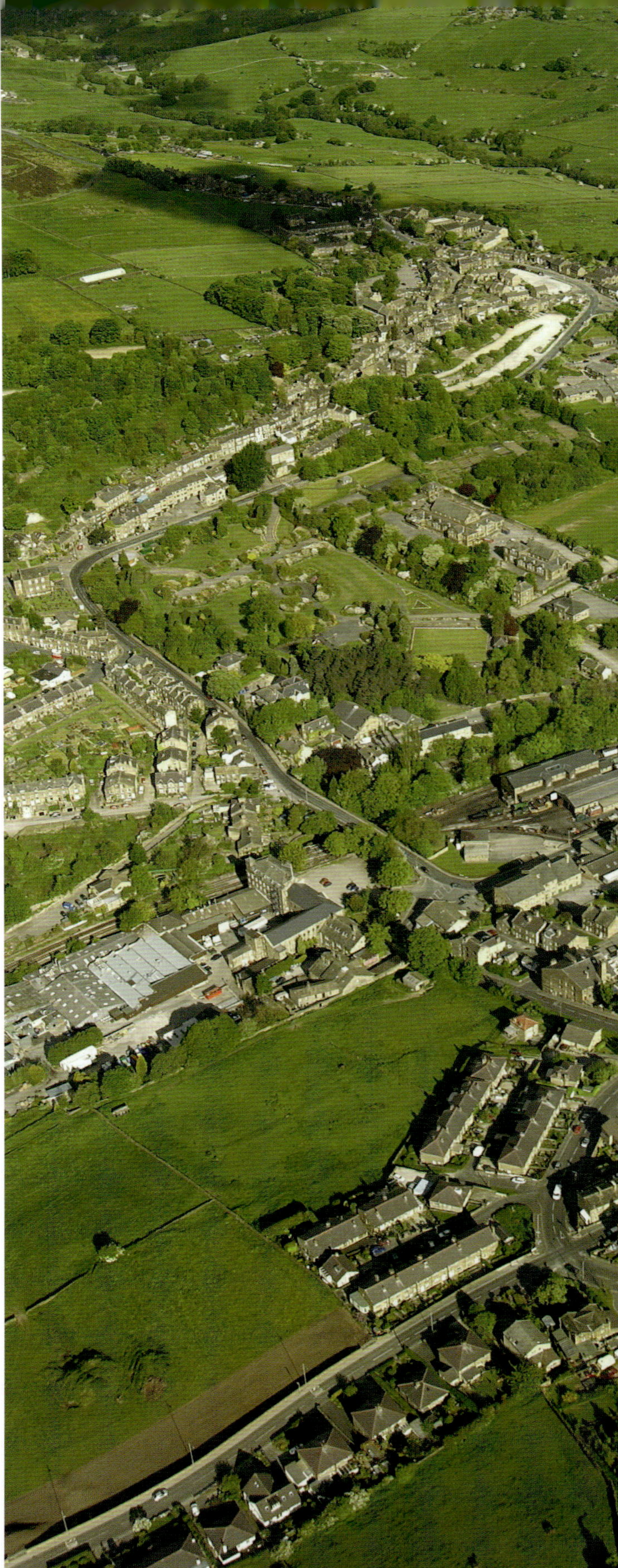

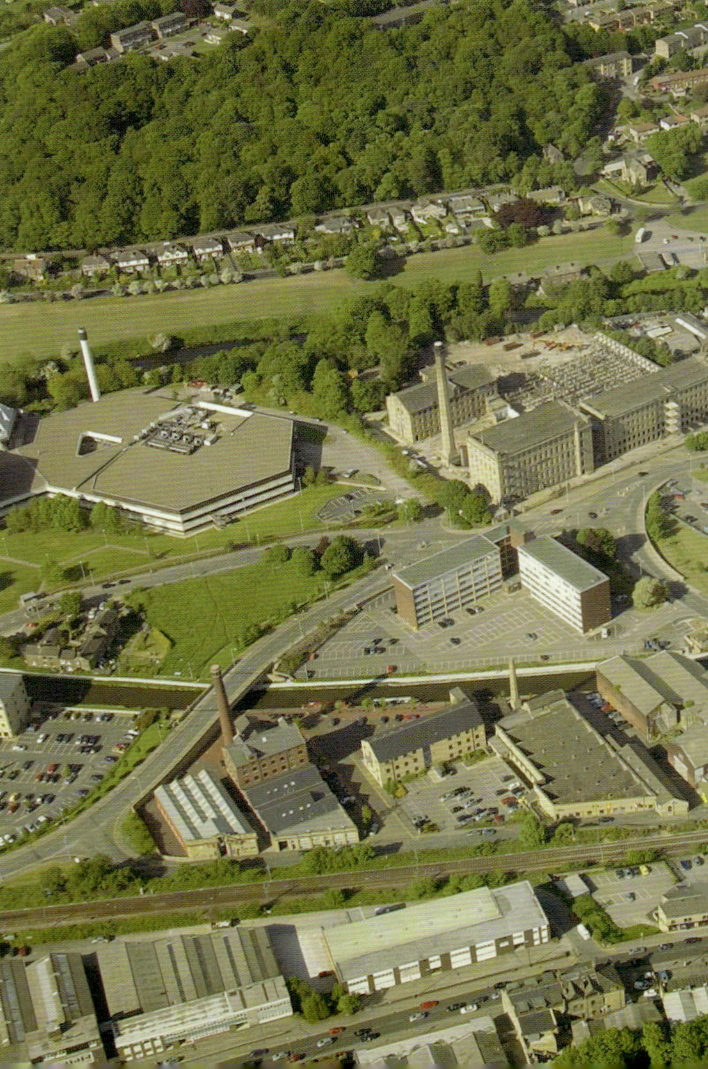

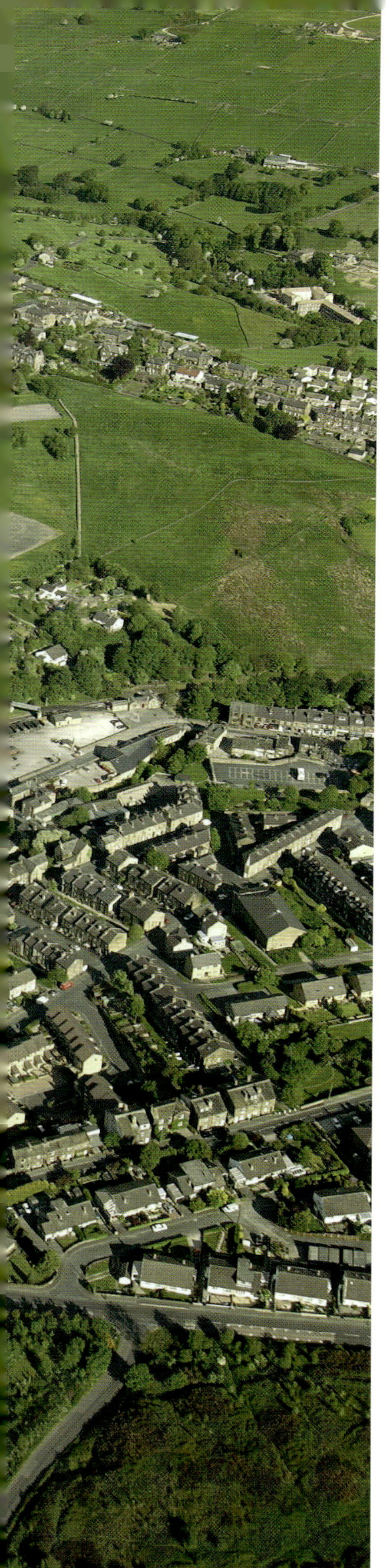

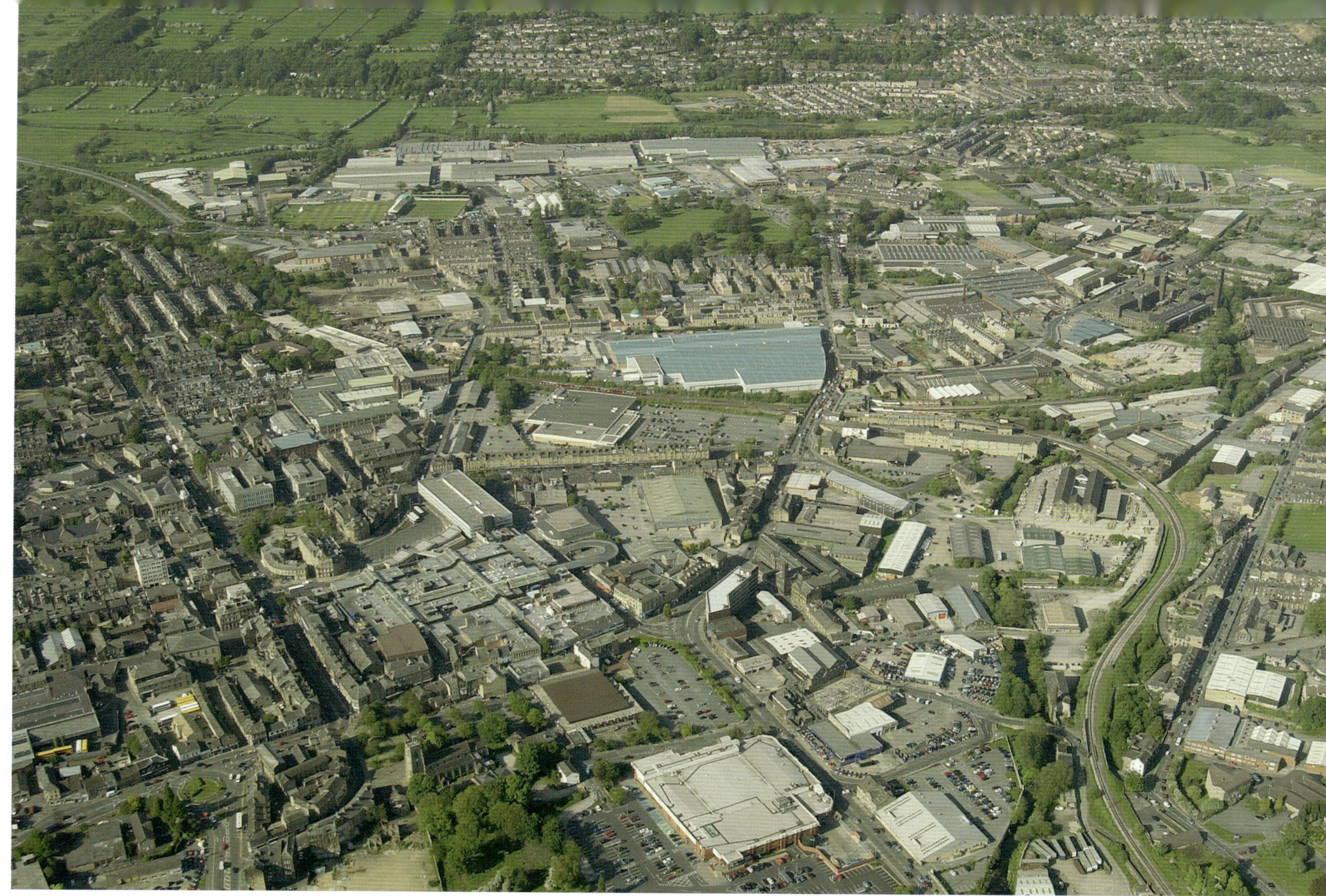

KEIGHLEY *(above)*

Keighley (pronounced Keith-ley, of course) grew up on the banks of the river Worth to the south of its confluence with the river Aire. It is best-known today for its railway station, the terminus for the steam trains that run on the Keighley & Worth Valley Railway which can be seen on the right. The view shows the industrial parts of the town beside the river Worth looking towards Eastwood and Aireworth with the town centre on the left. The blue roof is a large distribution centre.

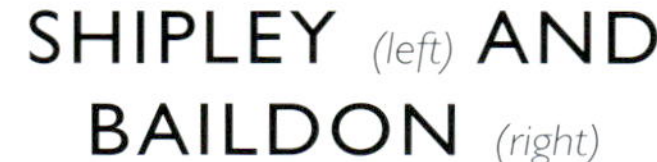

SHIPLEY *(left)* AND BAILDON *(right)*

Both of these small industrial towns in Airedale to the north of Bradford expanded initially because of their position beside the Leeds & Liverpool Canal. The photograph on the right is a view along the Aire valley north-eastwards from Shipley with much modern industrial development on the flat land beside the river, canal and railway in Baildon. The photograph on the left shows the northern part of Shipley just to the east of Saltaire beside the river Aire, the canal and the railway. Standing side by side between the river and canal are the Victoria Mills, currently being converted into luxury apartments, and the modern hexagonal-shaped Inland Revenue Accounts Office. Another interesting mill with its tall chimney stack, occupied by Aldon Brearley Print, stands between the bridge over the canal and the railway line towards the left-hand edge of the photograph.

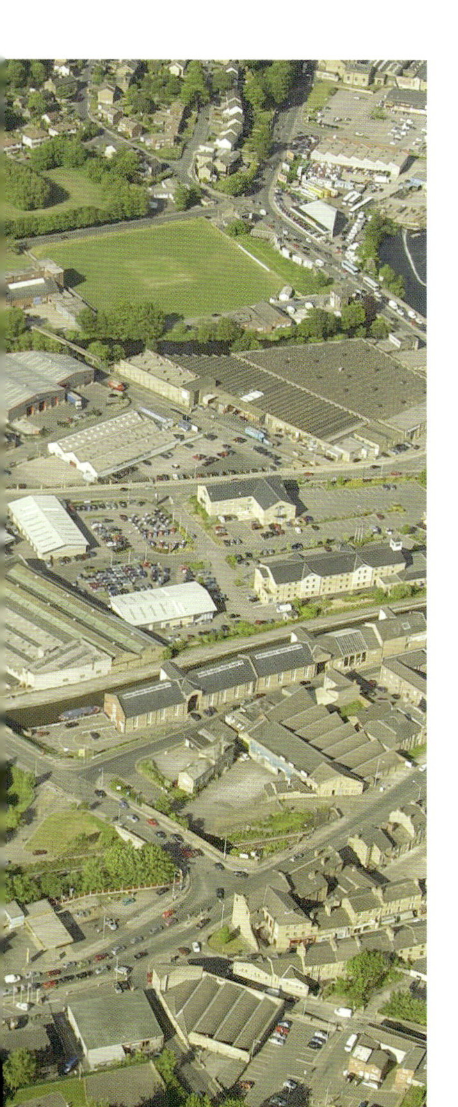

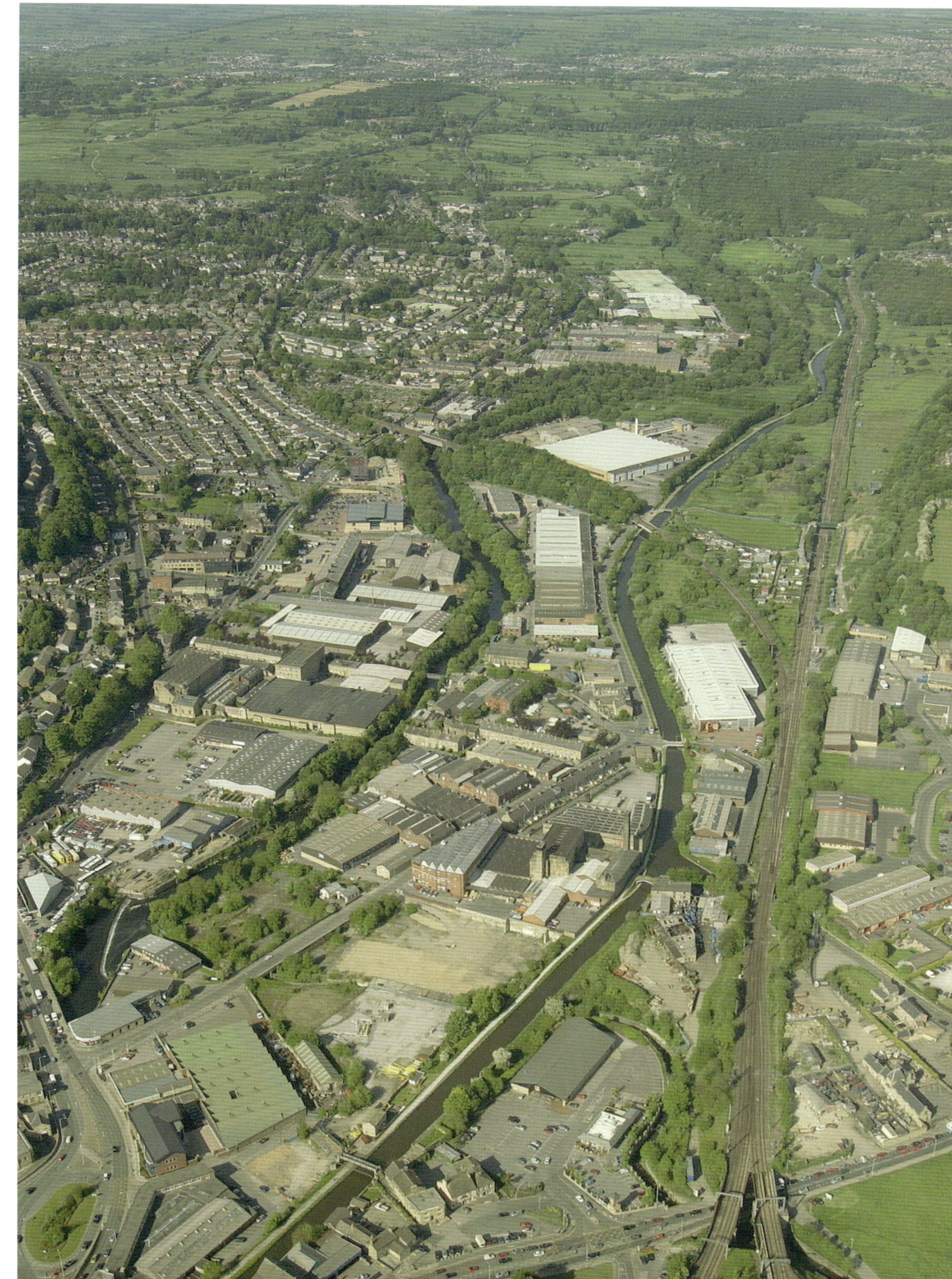

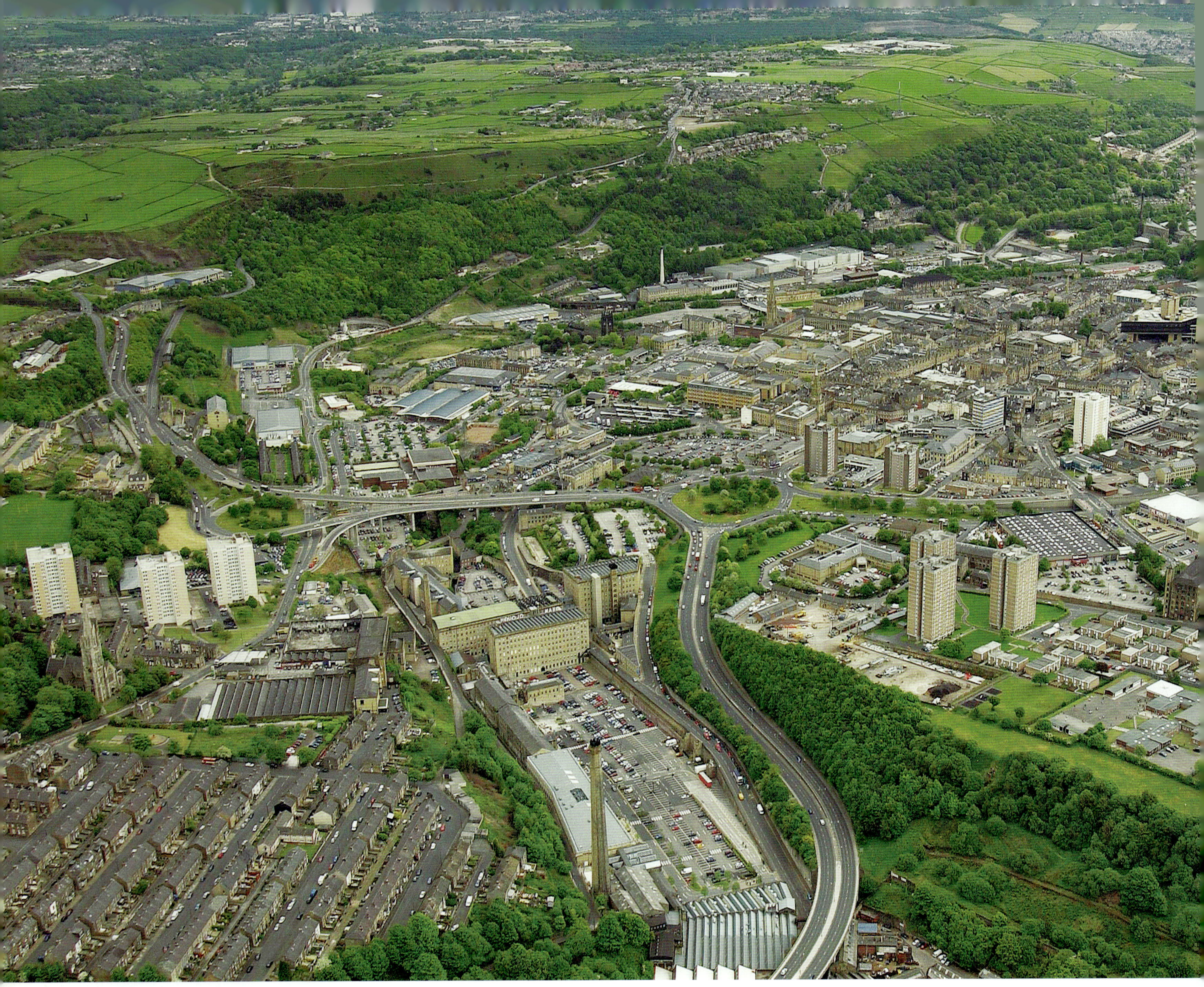

HALIFAX *(above and far right)*

Halifax originally grew up beside the river Hebble, a tributary of the river Calder, but with industrial development the town expanded in the direction of the Calder valley and the canal, and later the railway that linked it with Manchester and the port of Liverpool to the west and to the port of Hull to the east. The town has the distinction of having one of the earliest records of the wool textile industry in West Yorkshire: a carving of a pair of cloth shears in the porch of the parish church is thought to mark the burial place of a mid-12th century clothworker. The view above takes the eye along the Ovenden Road, past Dean Clough and over the town centre with the head office of Halifax plc (formerly the Halifax Building Society) and the Piece Hall as prominent features, to the wooded Hebble valley and Southowram beyond. Dean Clough is an arts, business, design and education complex created by Sir Ernest Hall and his son Jeremy from the derelict Dean Clough Mills, once one of the world's largest carpet factories. The photograph on the right is a view across the town from the south with the 253ft (77m) high Wainhouse Tower in the foreground.

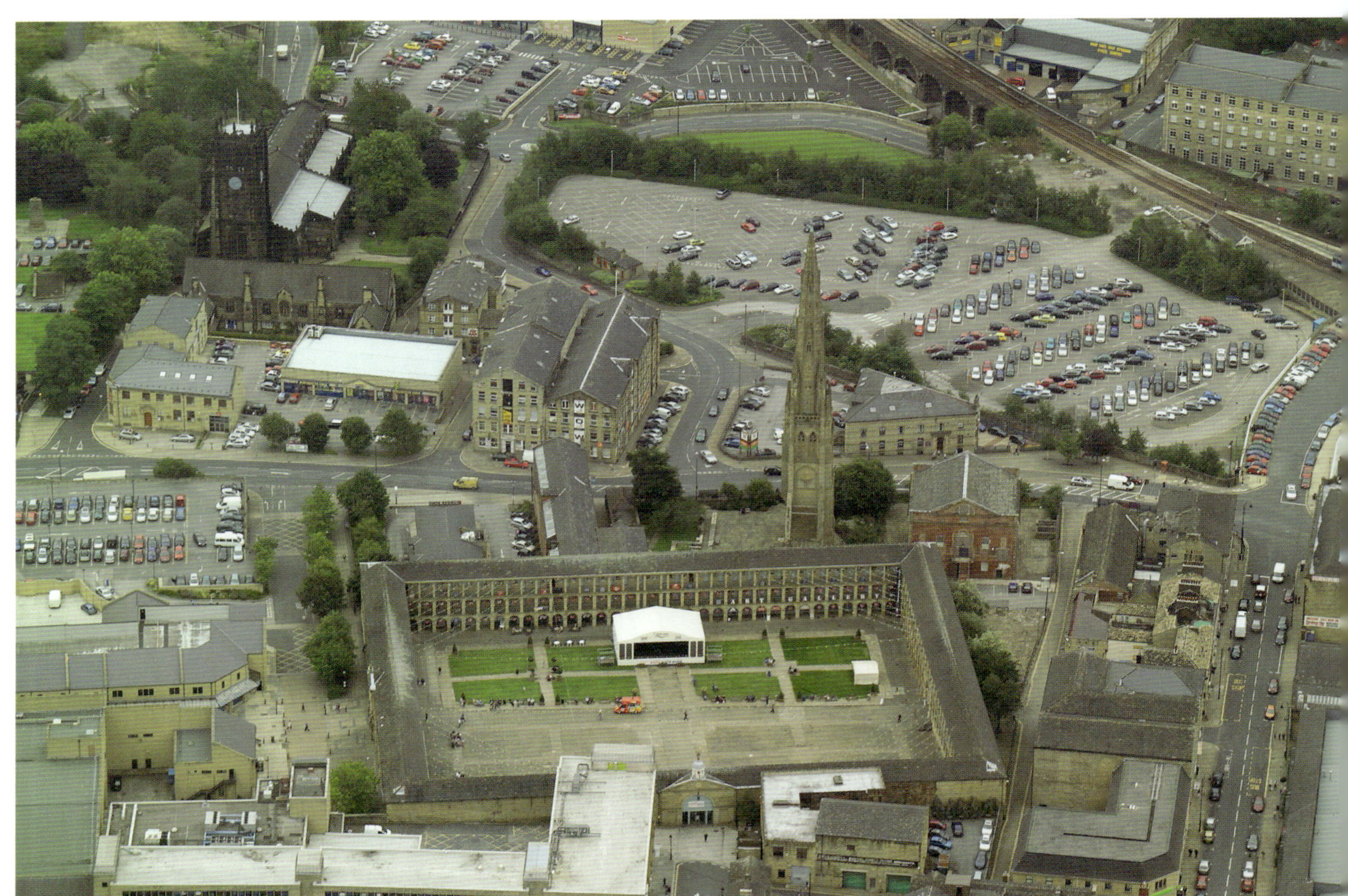

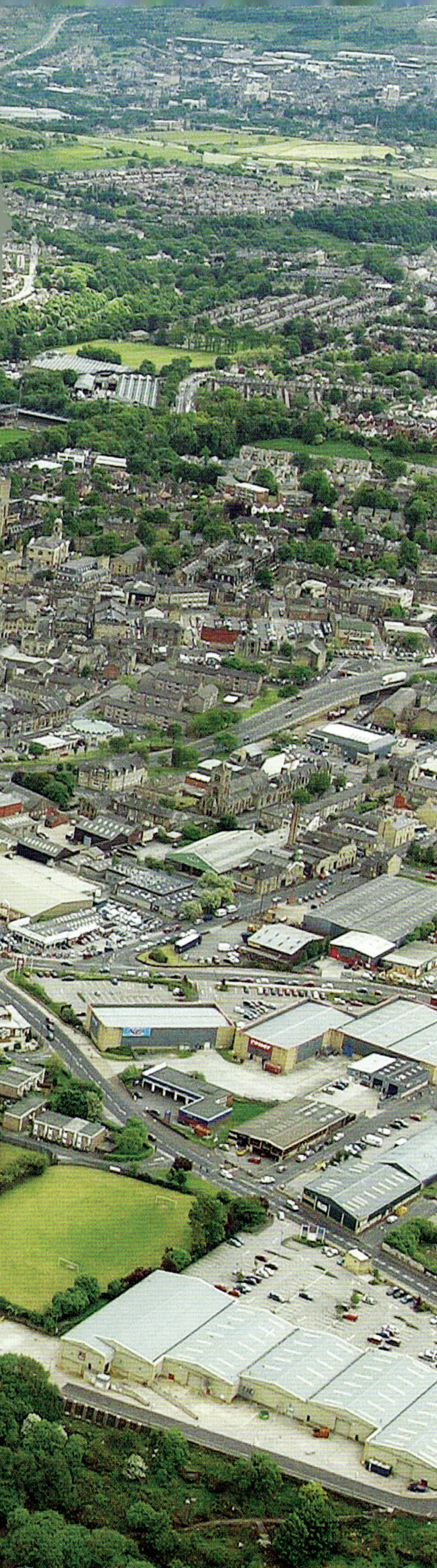

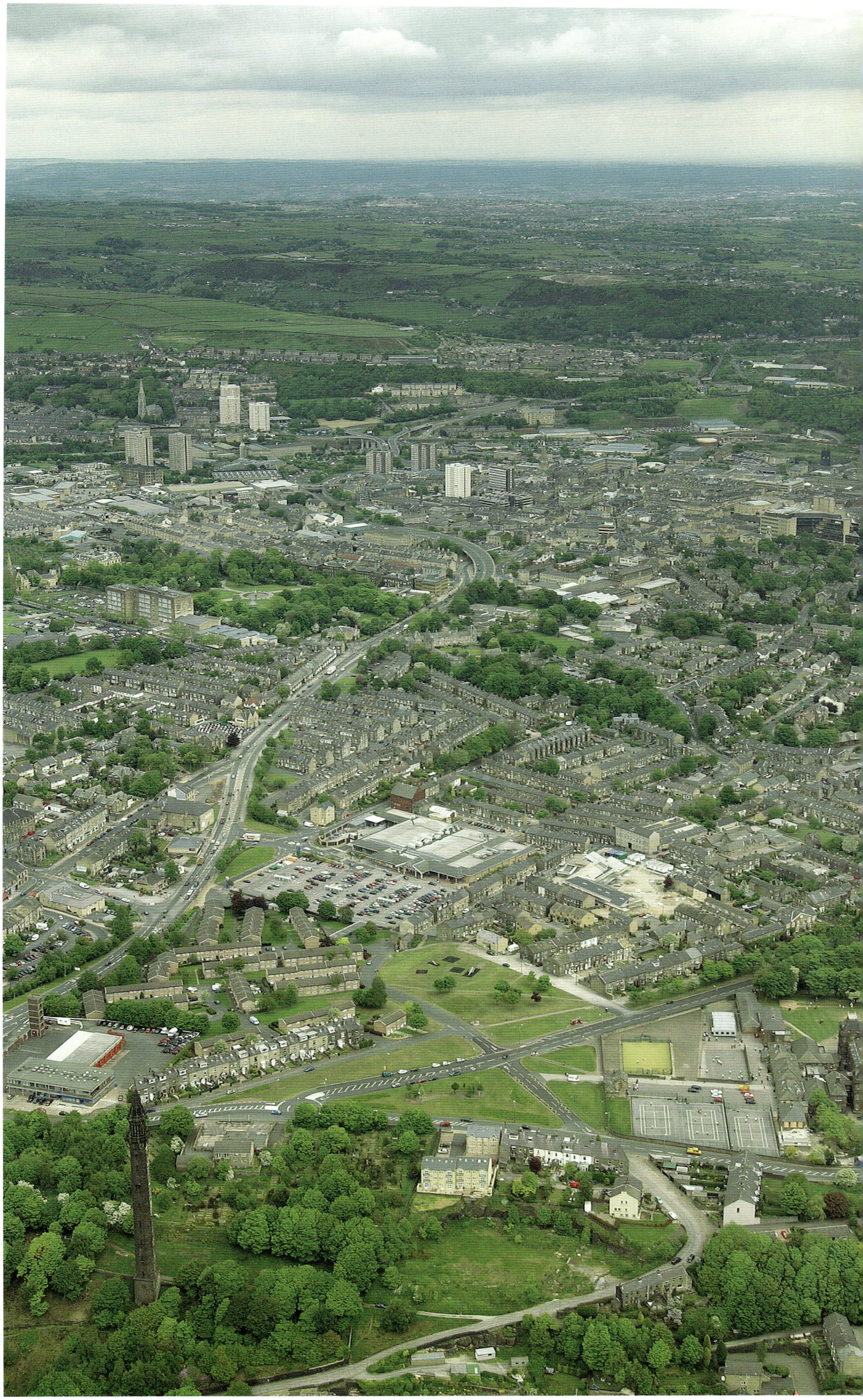

PIECE HALL, HALIFAX

(left)

This was a cloth hall, designed by John Hope of Liverpool, completed in 1779, to which handloom weavers brought their "pieces" of woollen cloth for sale, hence its name. The more than 300 rooms of the cloth hall are built around an open quadrangle which is entered through a grand archway. From the quadrangle, 90,000sq ft (8,361sq m) in size, on all sides rise the galleried arcades, with rusticated square pillars below and Tuscan columns above. The Piece Hall became a wholesale vegetable and fish market in the 1870s. It was renovated in 1976 and now contains a variety of shops and an art gallery, and the quadrangle is the venue for a weekly flea market and a general market.

HEADQUARTERS OF HALIFAX PLC *(below)*

Standing in Commercial Street is this unforgettable and, for many residents and visitors, visually unattractive, late 20th-century architectural monster. It was designed by the Building Design Partnership and completed in 1975 for the then Halifax Building Society. In the shape of a giant diamond it stands on concrete legs and dwarfs the town's earlier private and public buildings.

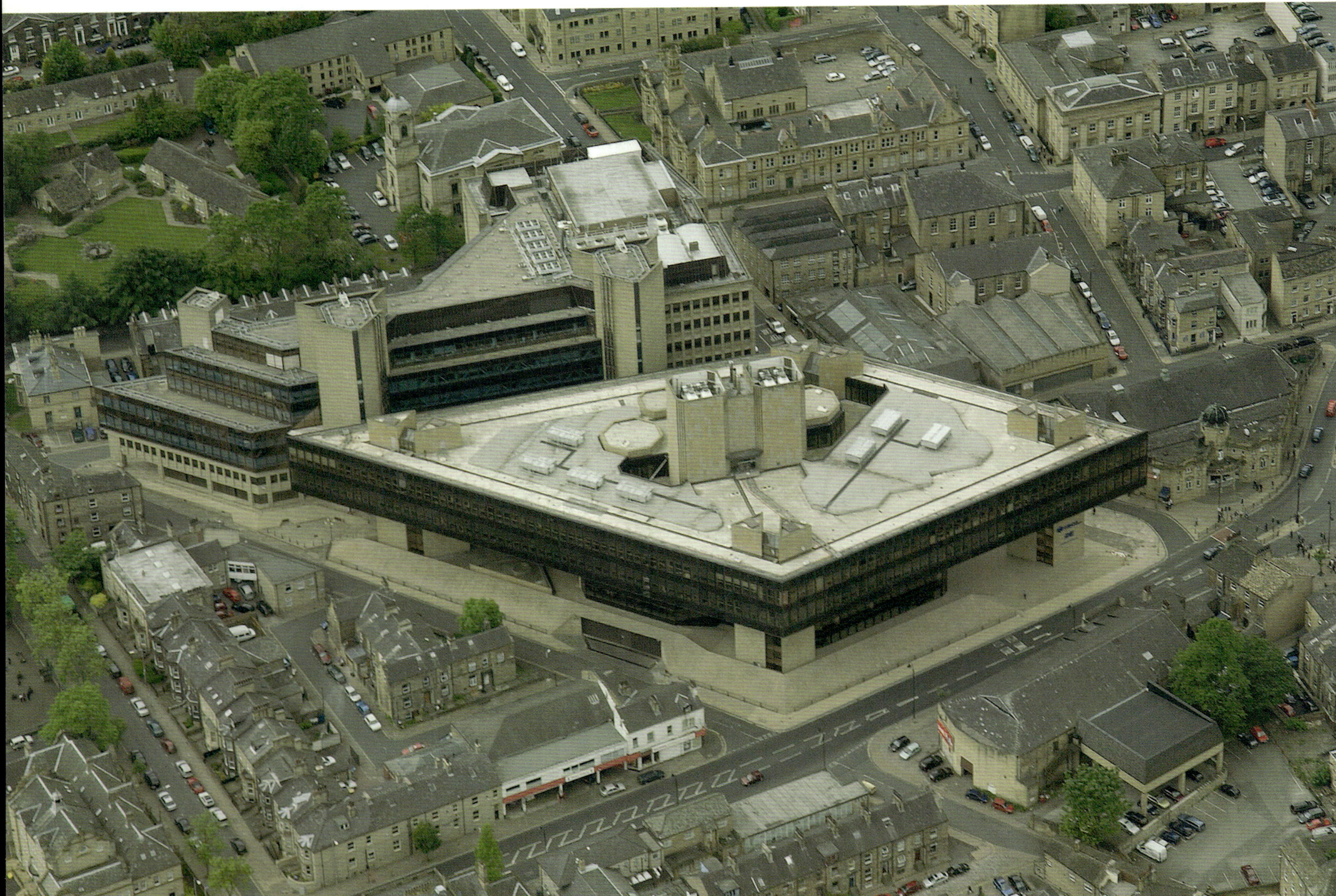

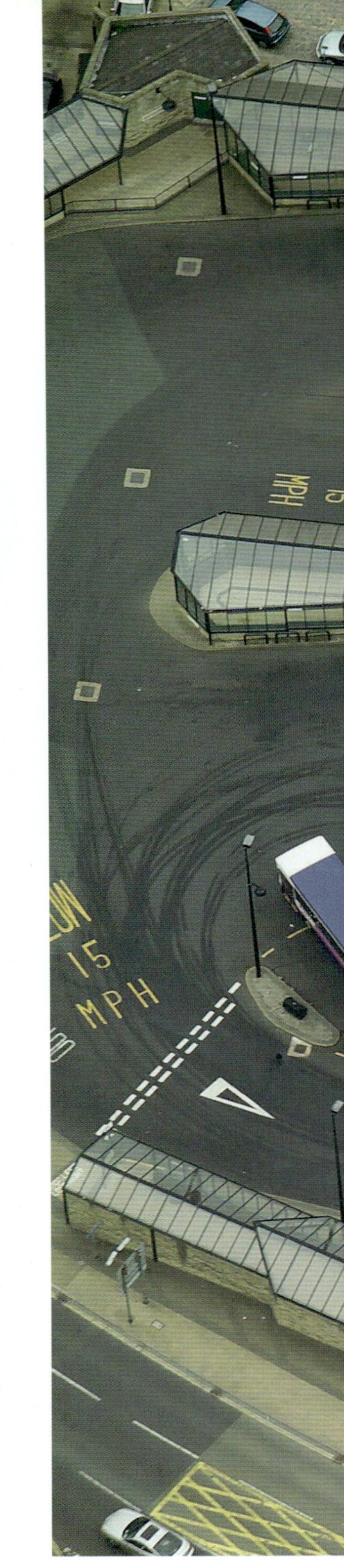

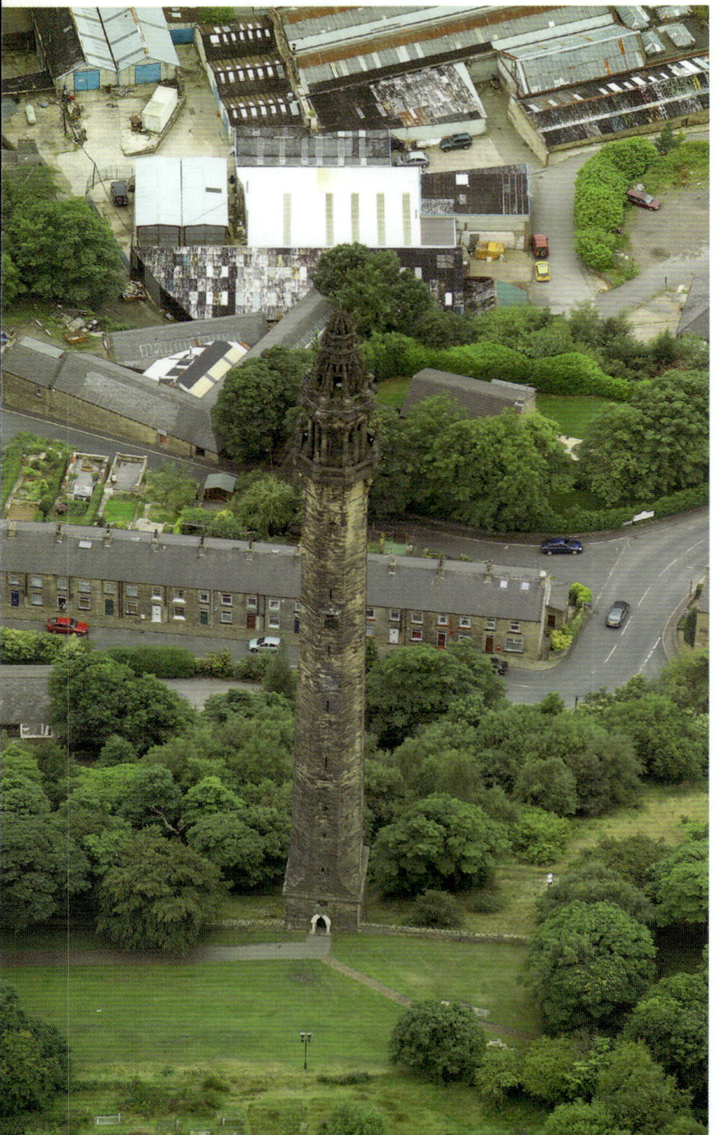

WAINHOUSE TOWER, HALIFAX

(left)

This tower is the product of the Smoke Abatement Act of 1870. It was built for John Edward Wainhouse, the wealthy owner of Washer Lane Dye Works. As a result of the Act it became necessary to construct a tall chimney to carry the smoke and fumes from the works out of the Calder valley. The chimney was to be connected to the works by means of a pipeline. Before it was completed Wainhouse sold the works but decided to keep the tower and turn it into an astronomical observatory. It is 253ft (77m) high and richly decorated at the top with balustrades, finials and other fantastical carvings. It is said that one reason why it was built was that Wainhouse was in dispute with his neighbour Sir Harry Edwards, who did not like chimneys, and it enabled him to anger Edwards and at the same time keep a close eye on what he was up to.

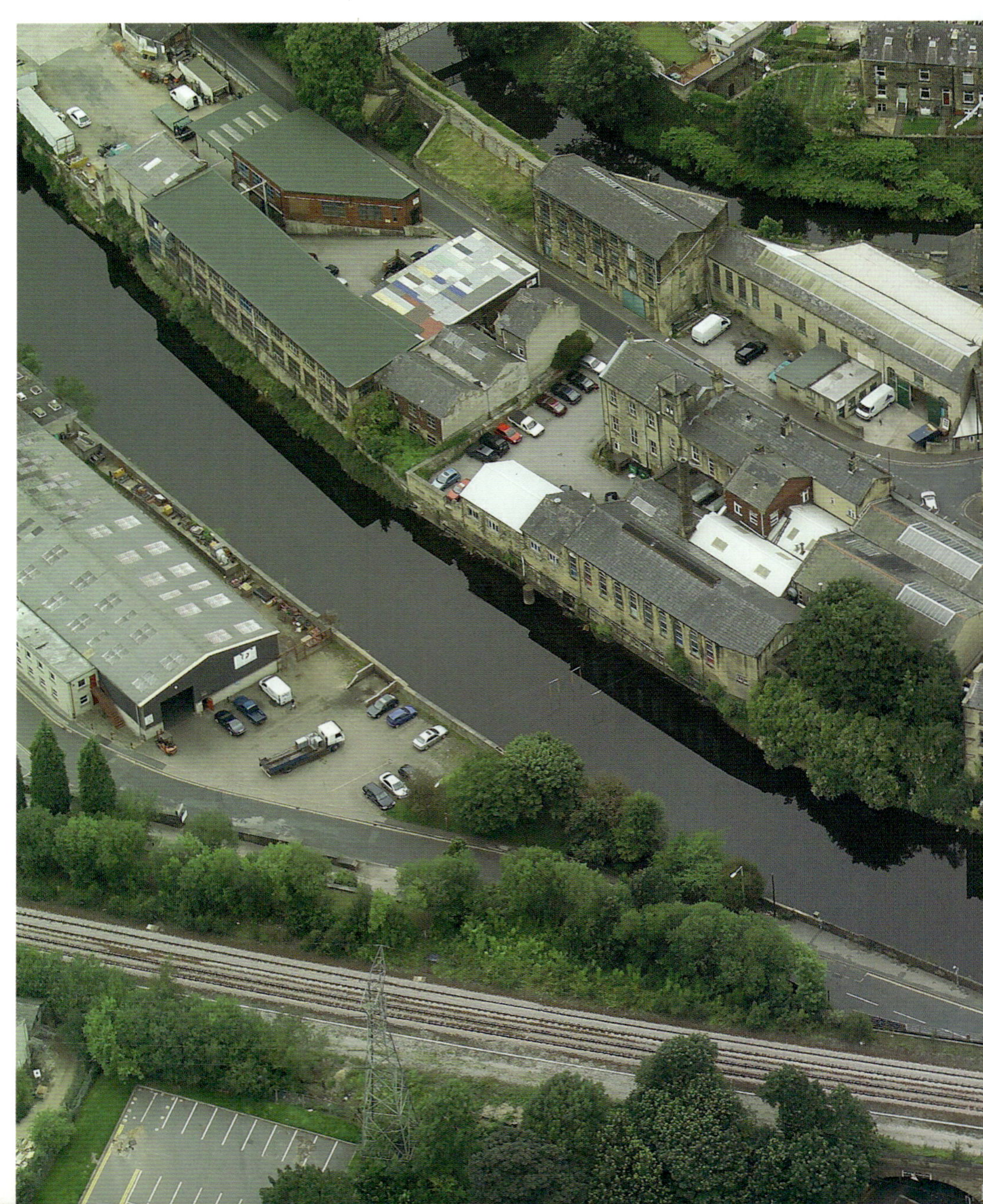

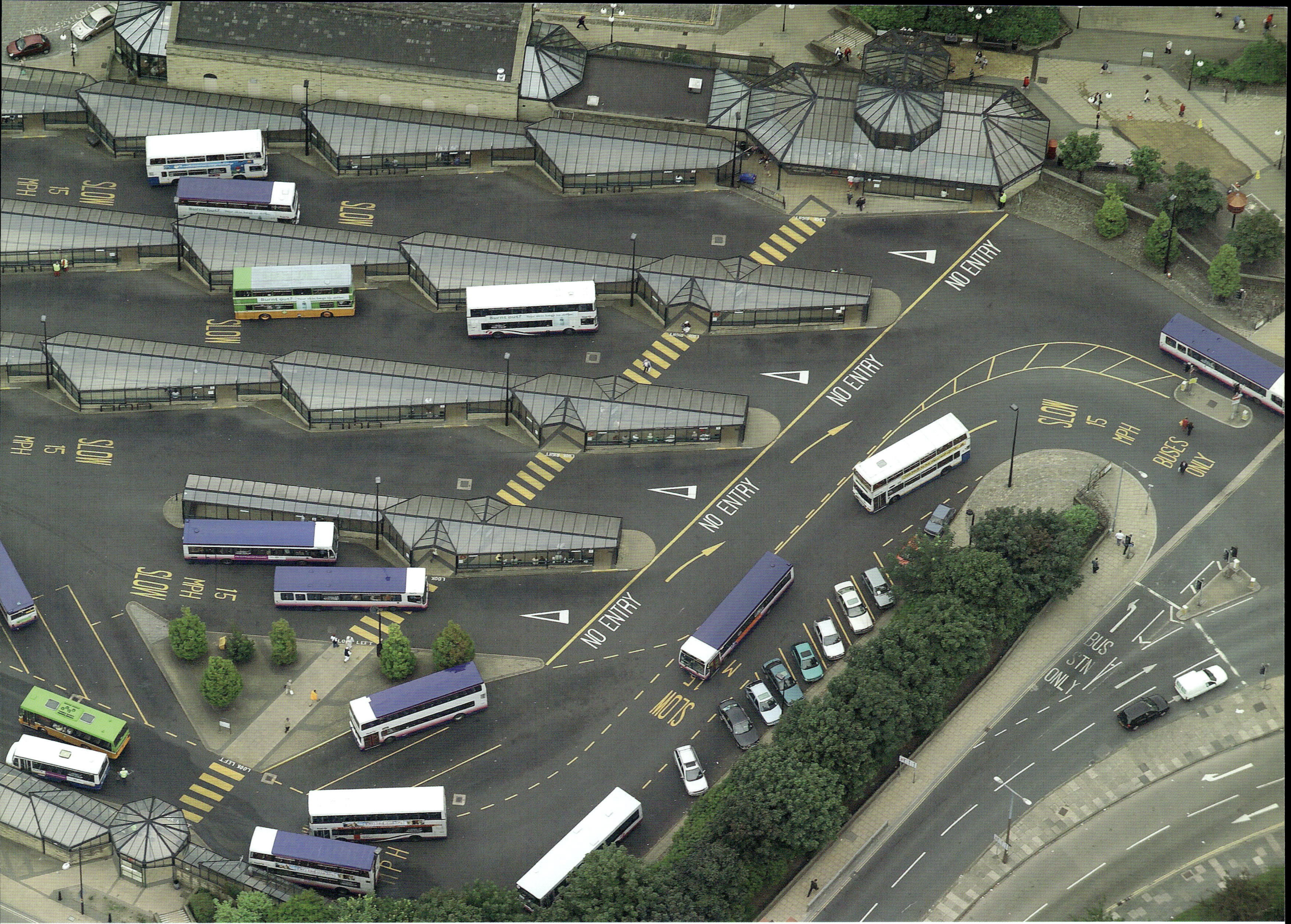

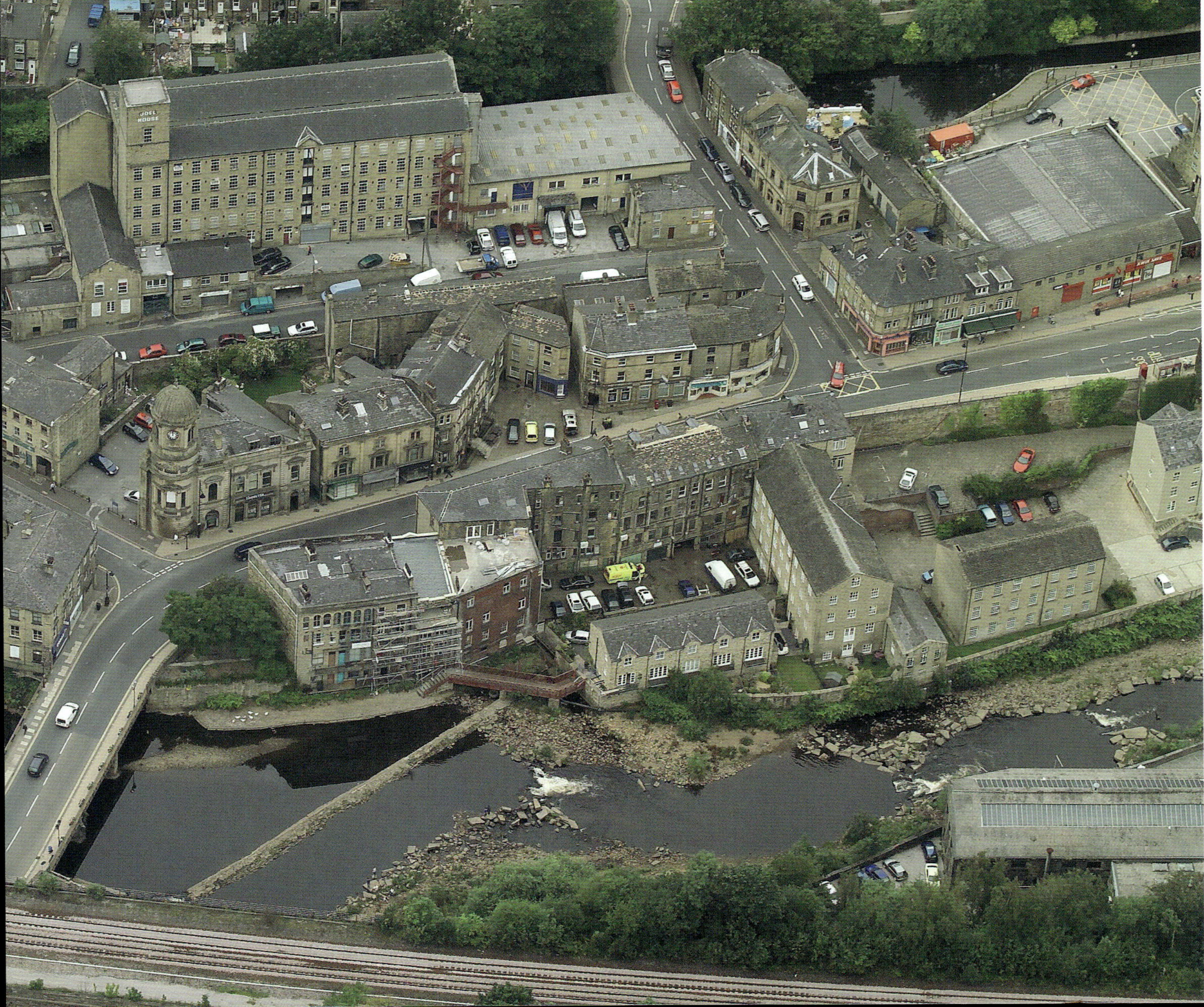

HALIFAX BUS STATION *(above)* AND SOWERBY BRIDGE *(left)*

Buses leave Halifax bus station for the surrounding towns and villages such as Mytholmroyd, Luddenden Foot, Hipperholme – and Sowerby Bridge. Originally the villages of the area grew up on shelves of grit above the valley floors and had the appearance of hill villages. Spinning and weaving were domestic processes carried out in the hill settlements. Two processes needed water-power – washing and beating the cloth to remove dirt and grease, and thickening and felting, both of which were carried out at a fulling mill in the river valley. All this changed in the 18th and 19th centuries when spinning and weaving were done by water power and then steam power and canals and railways came to the area through the valleys. The settlements around the fulling mills then expanded into manufacturing towns and the hill settlements became industrial museums. Sowerby Bridge is one of these creations of the Industrial Revolution. Others include Hebden Bridge (an offshoot of Heptonstall) and Brighouse (an offshoot from Raistrick). The photograph shows not only the bridge but also the river, the canal, the railway and a textile mill.

HUDDERSFIELD *(below, top right and bottom right)*

The product of the development of the woollen industry, Huddersfield occupies the valleys of the Calder, Colne and Holme and the surrounding hillsides and plateaus. But it was the river valleys that attracted the industrial development in the 18th and 19th centuries and led to the rapid expansion of the town. The initial attractions were the rivers themselves and the use of water-power. In the valleys canals were then built and later the railways, that brought coal to fuel the steam-engines that superseded water-wheels, and transported the raw material and the finished product. Below is the valley of the river Holme near Lockwood, looking towards the Calder valley and beyond to the centre of Huddersfield. In the background on the Leeds Road can be seen the distinctive shape of the McAlpine Stadium, the home of Huddersfield Town FC and Huddersfield Giants rugby league club. In the foreground can be seen the 36-arch Lockwood viaduct built in 1846-48 on the railway line to Sheffield. Dominating the town centre in the photographs immediately to the right is the railway station built in 1847-48 in the Classical Corinthian style. Opposite the railway station is the George hotel, the birthplace of rugby league in 1895.

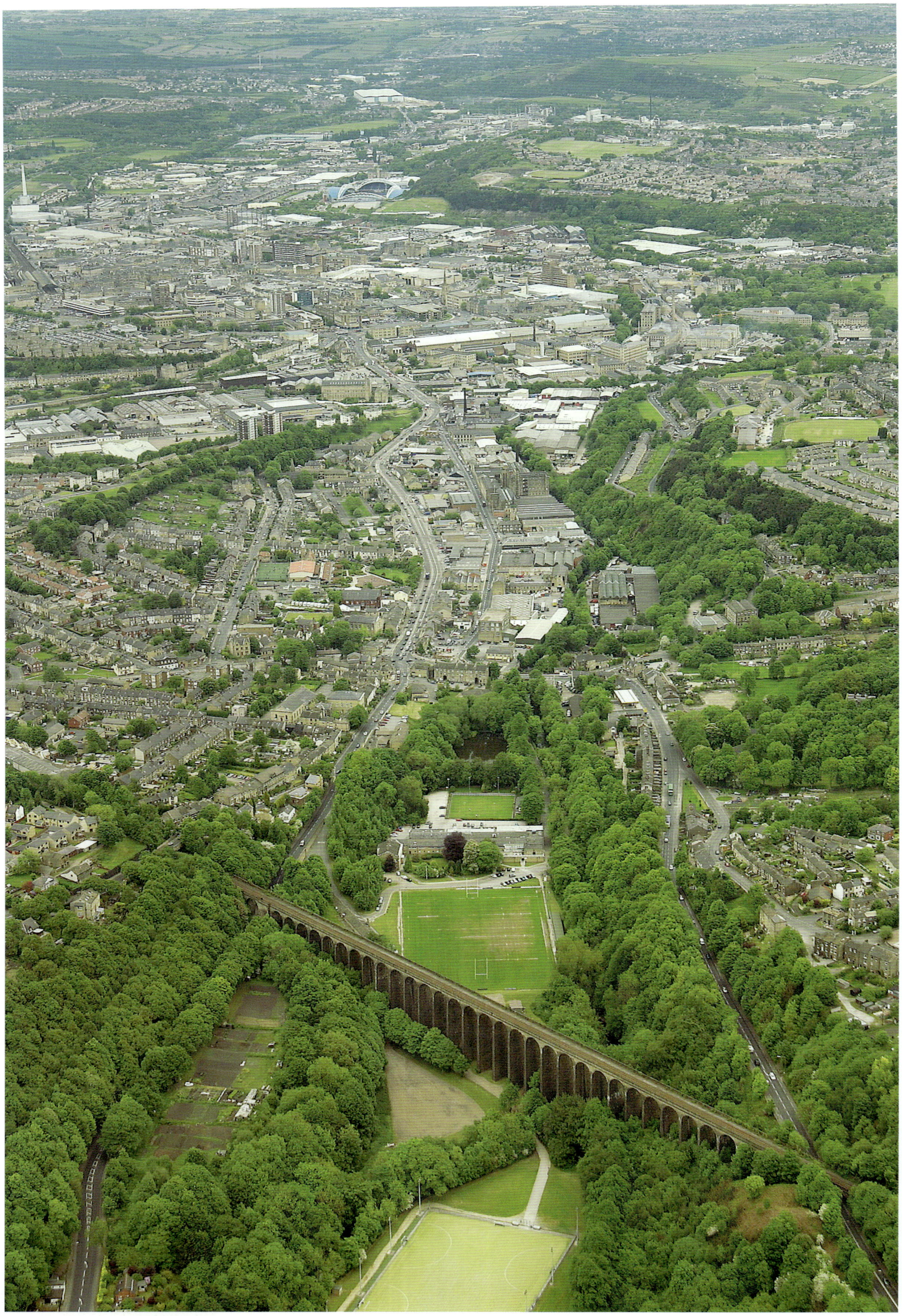

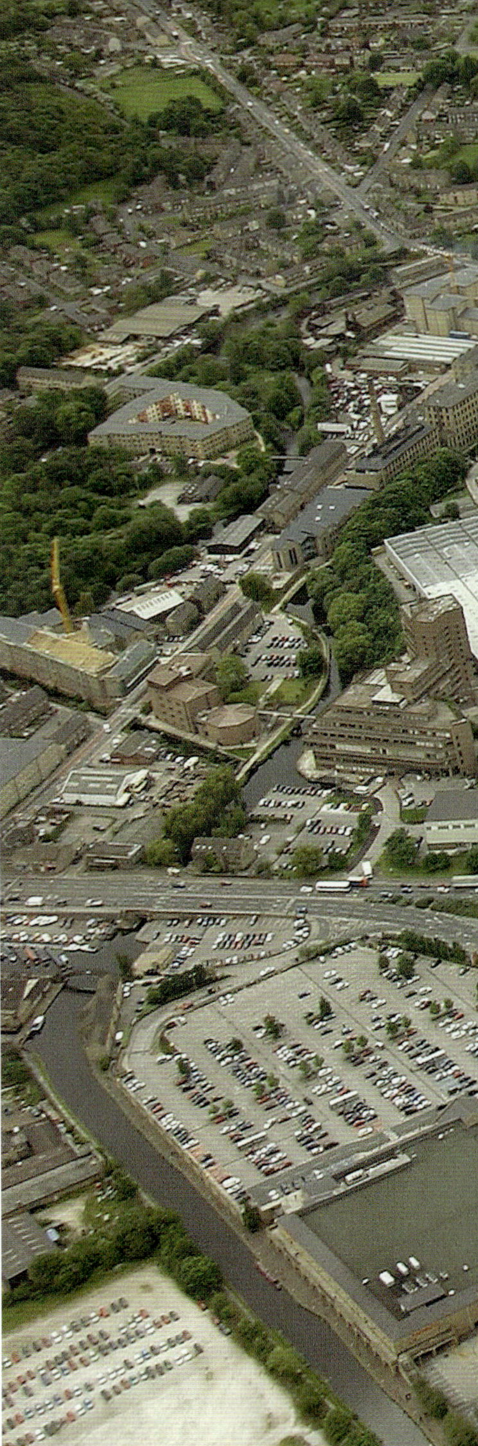

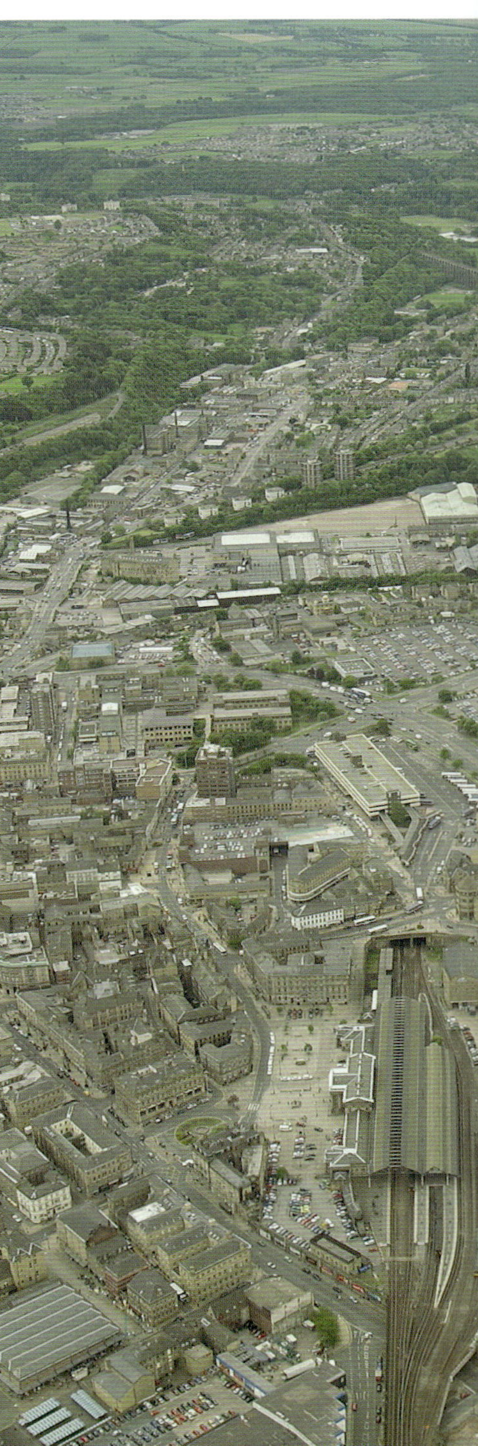

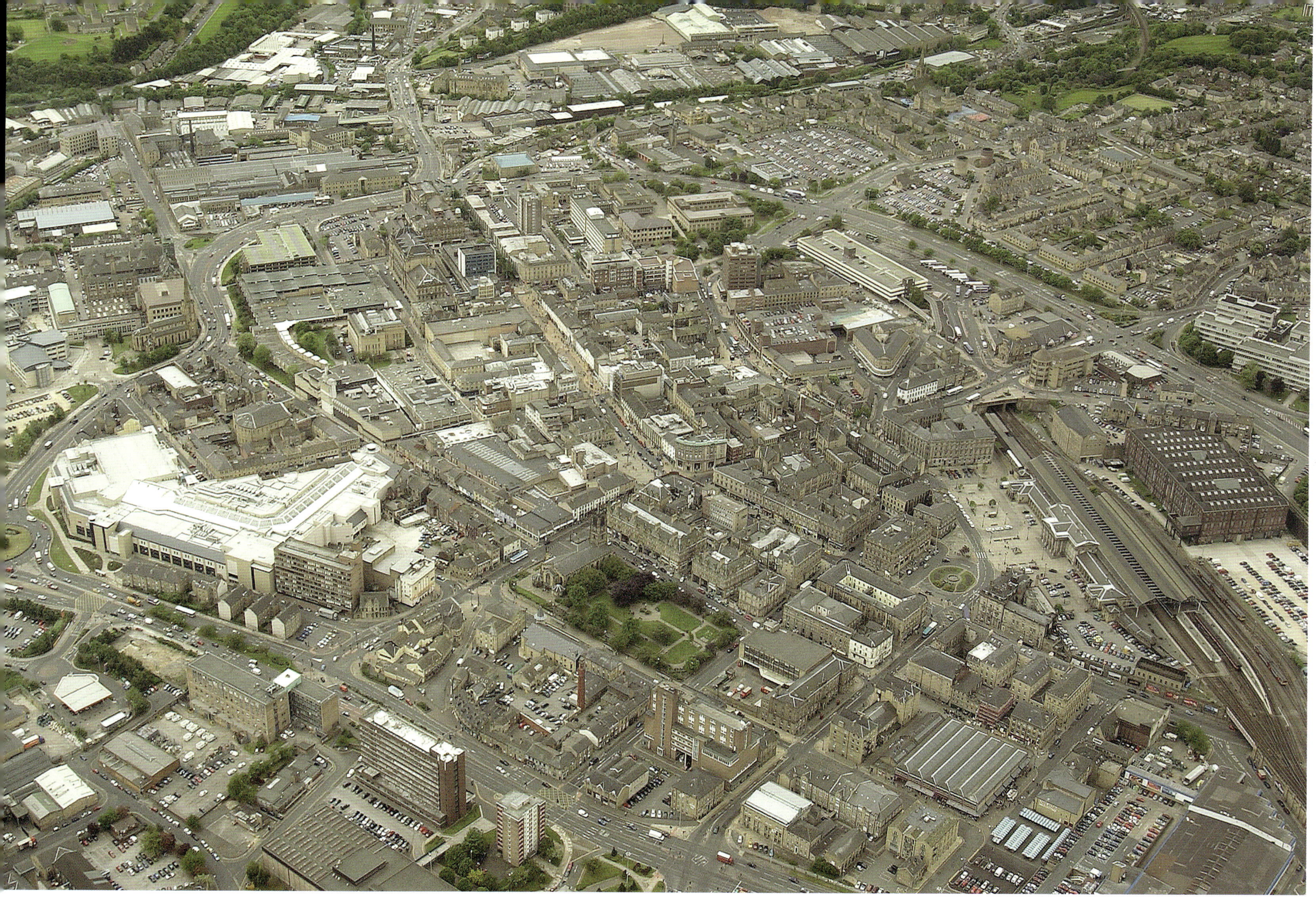

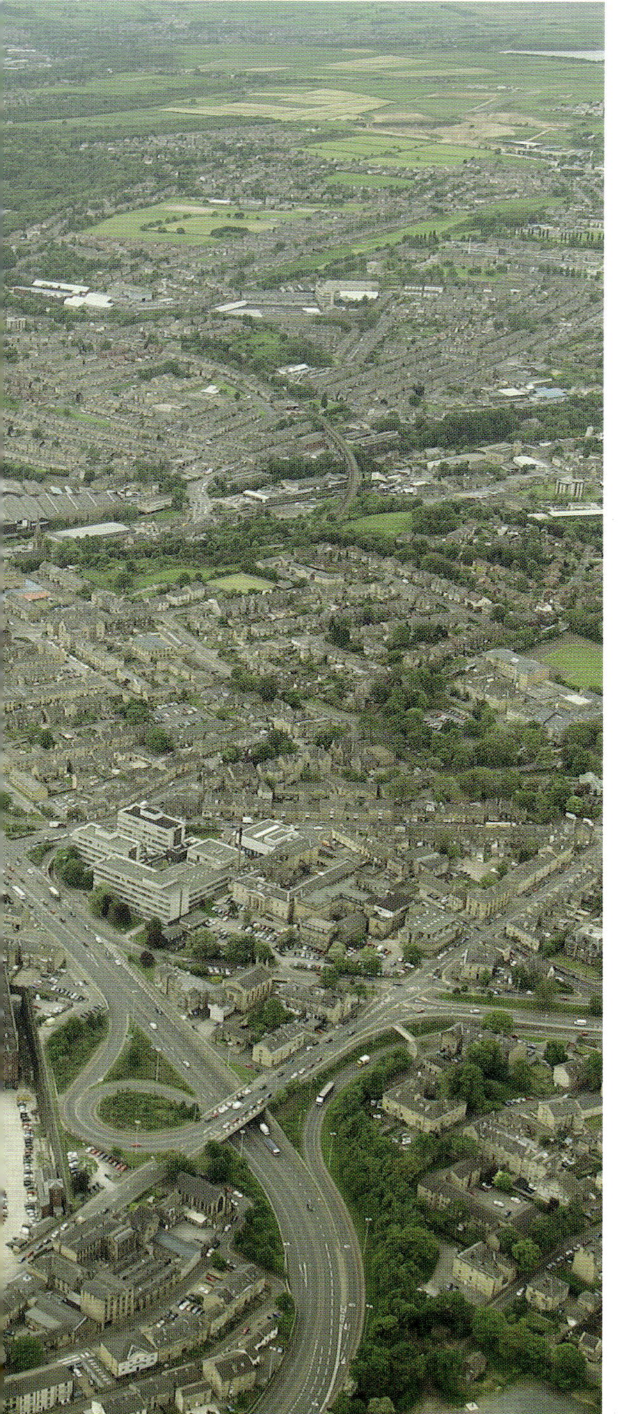

VICTORIA TOWER, ALMONDBURY

Crowning the gorse-covered Castle Hill, which is steep on three of its four sides and rises to 800ft (244m), is an Iron Age camp which is believed to have begun to be constructed in about 300BC by the Brigantian tribe. Originally it consisted of a single stone rampart, but this was later doubled and then a third outer rampart was added. It is assumed to have been abandoned with the coming of the Romans. In the reign of King Stephen (1135-1154) a stone keep was built on the hilltop that was later demolished by King Henry III (1216-1272). The top of Castle Hill is now occupied by the Victoria Tower built in 1897-98 to celebrate Queen Victoria's diamond jubilee. From its turreted rooftop at the top of a stairway of 165 steps can be seen the glorious views of the surrounding countryside which is typical "stone country": stone cottages, stone-walled fields and extensive woodlands. To the west the views stretch to the high Pennine moorlands and to the north over the industrialised Colne valley into central Huddersfield. On a windy day this is a wonderful place to get rid of the cobwebs!

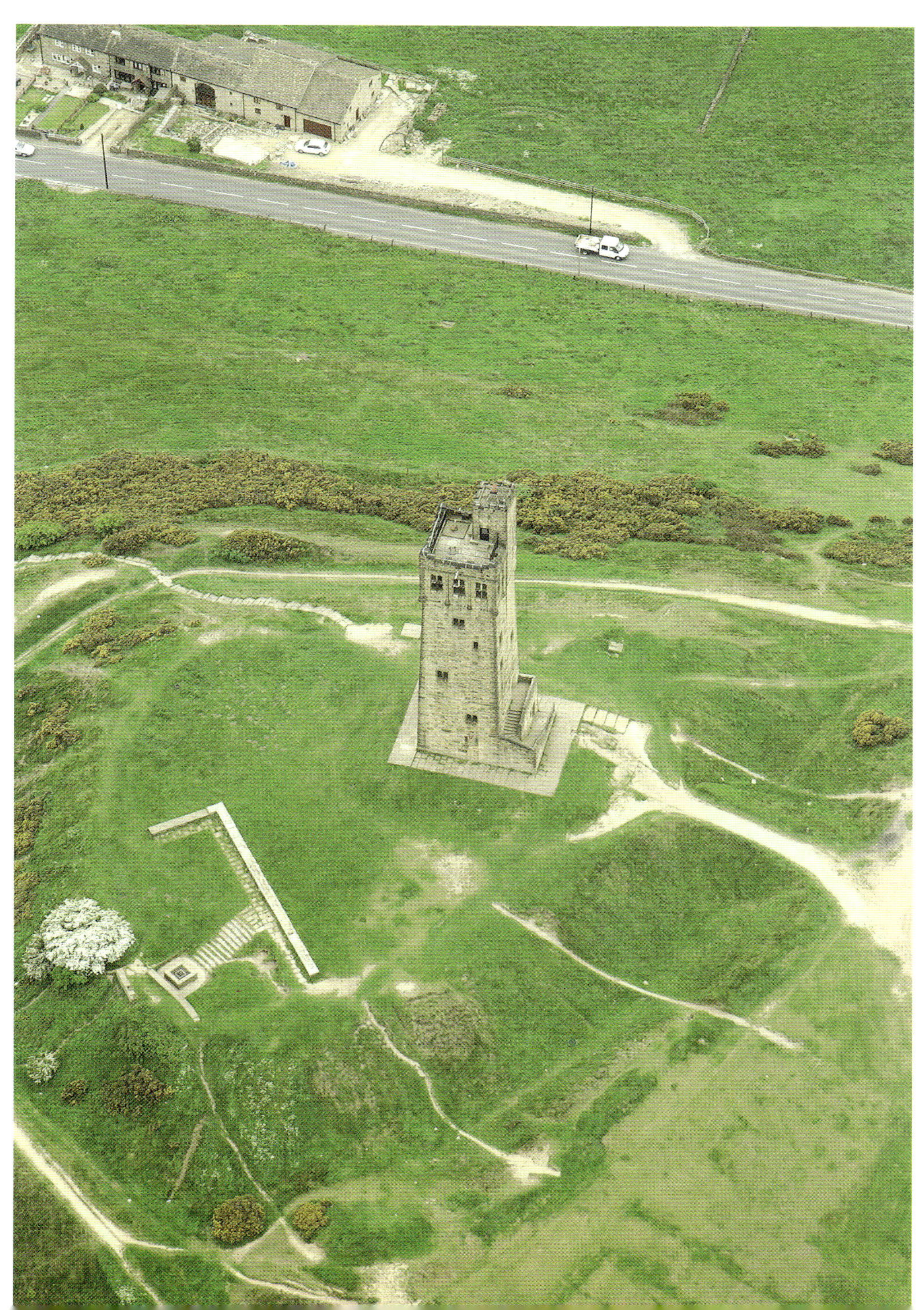

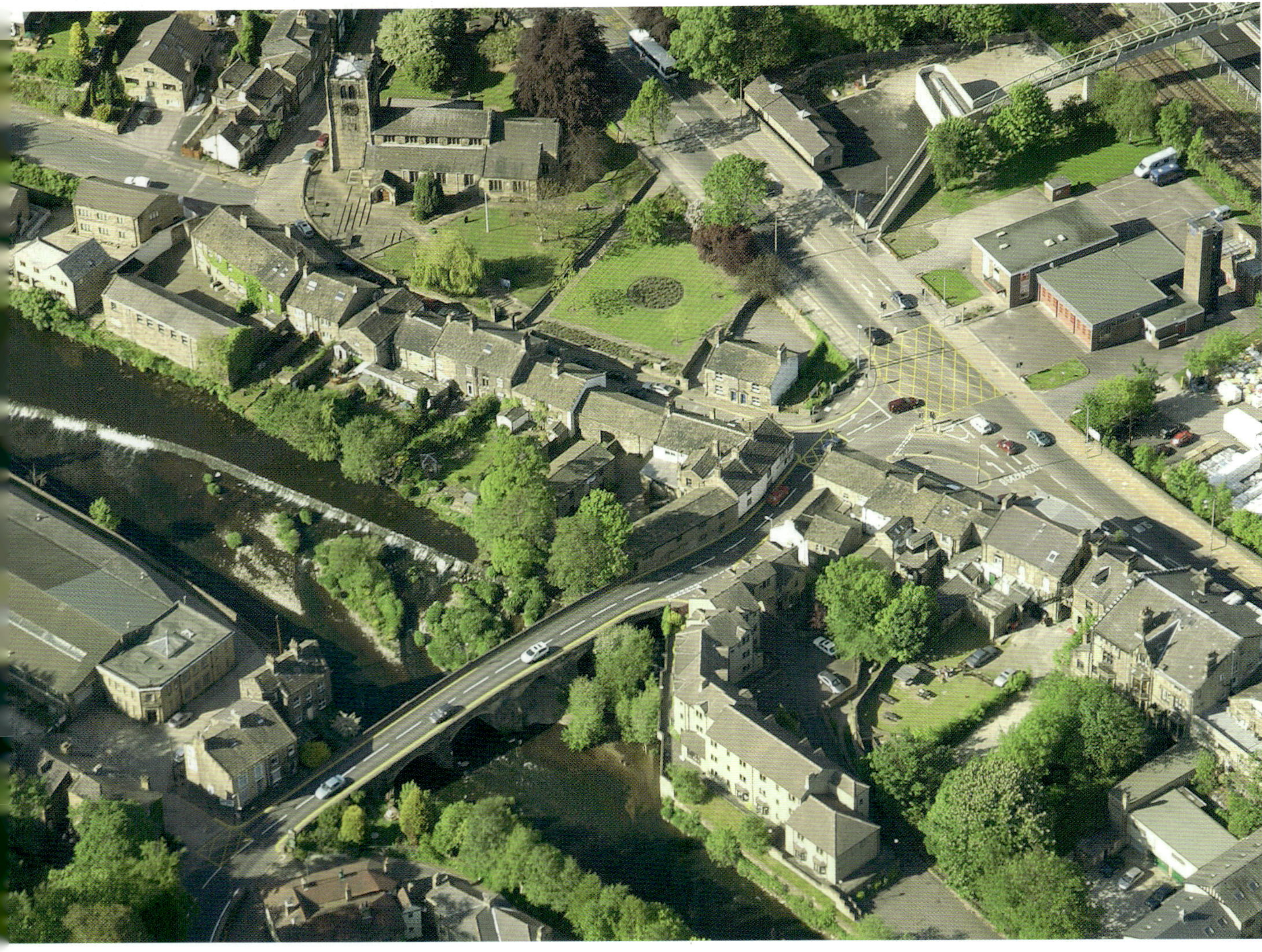

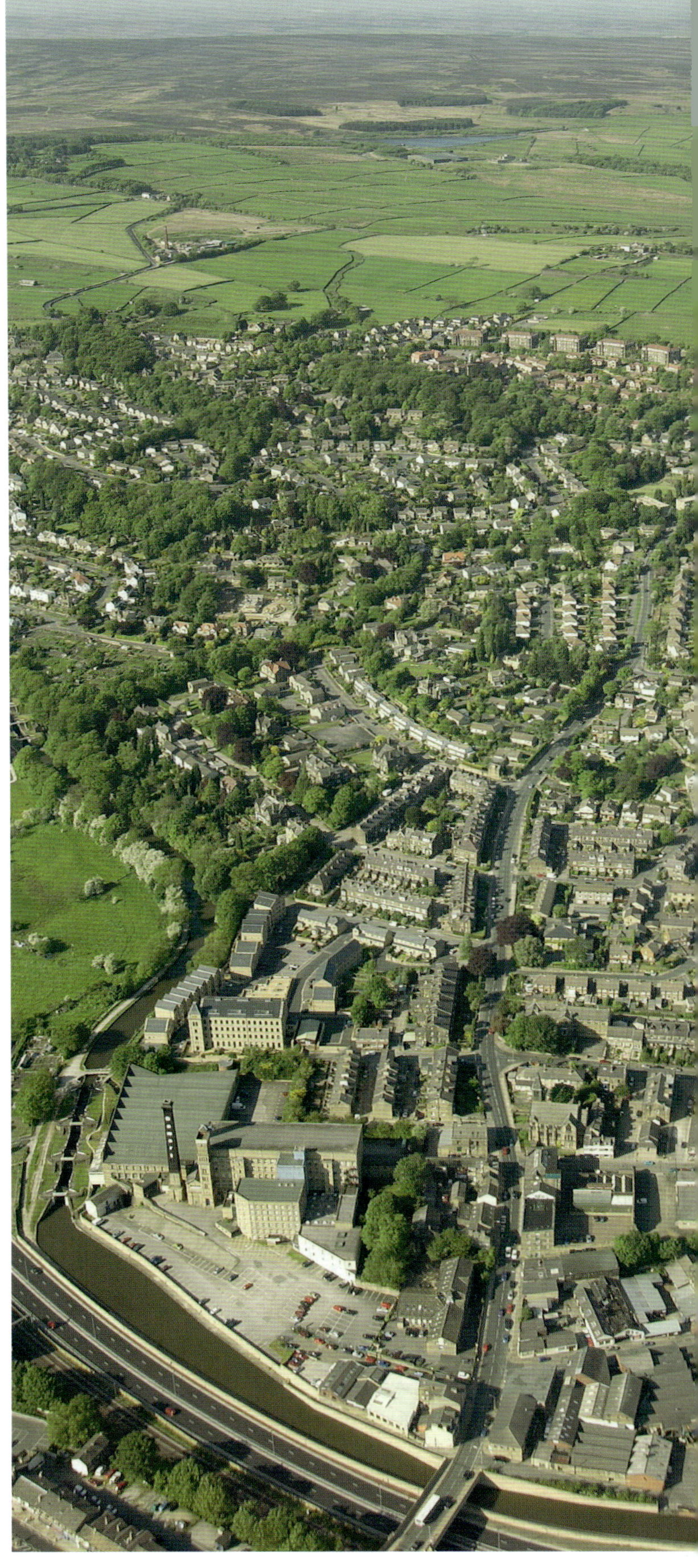

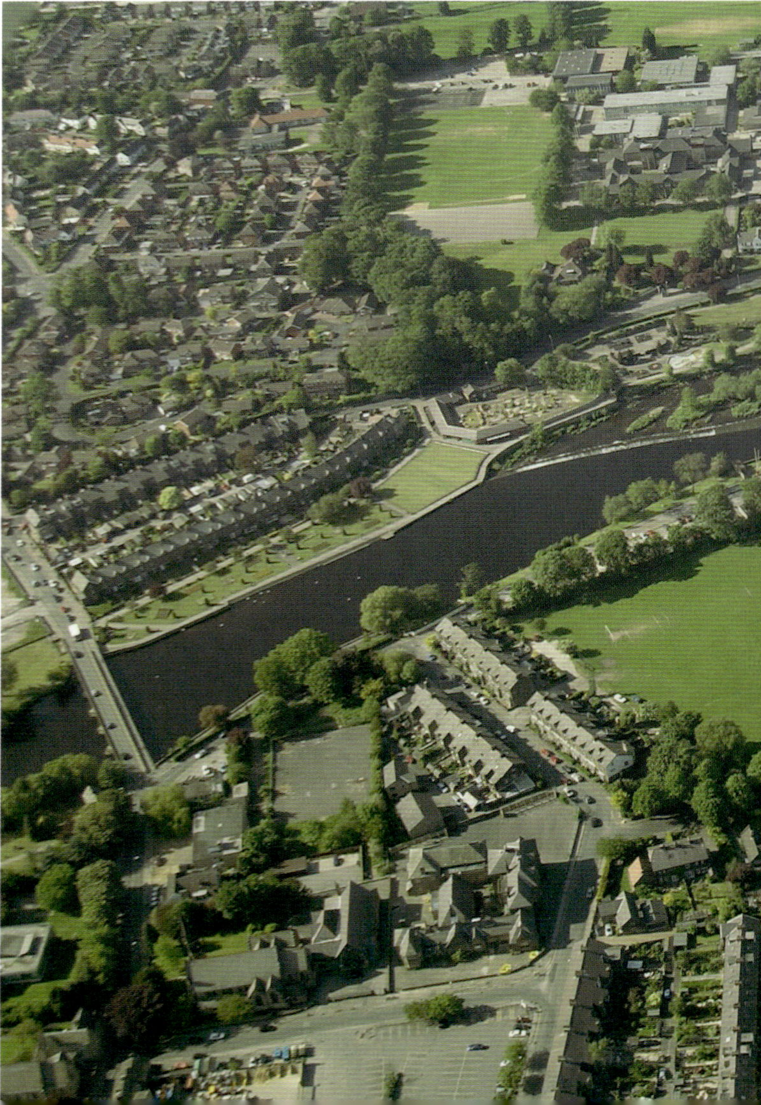

BINGLEY *(above, right and far right)*

Bingley was granted a market charter in 1212 by King John and after going through a long industrial phase is now a thriving commuter town for Bradford. The town was the place of residence of Sir Titus Salt's son – Titus Salt junior – who had his mansion built (now demolished) at Milner Field in 1873. The photograph on the far right shows a view over the town along the A650 and the Leeds and Liverpool Canal in the direction of Shipley and Bradford. The photograph on the right shows the Park Road bridge crossing of the railway, the A650 and the Leeds and Liverpool Canal on the southern edge of the town. The Prince of Wales Park can be seen in the background on the northern outskirts of the town. The photograph above shows Ireland Bridge over the river Aire. This stone bridge, built in 1686 and widened in 1776, replaced an earlier timber bridge.

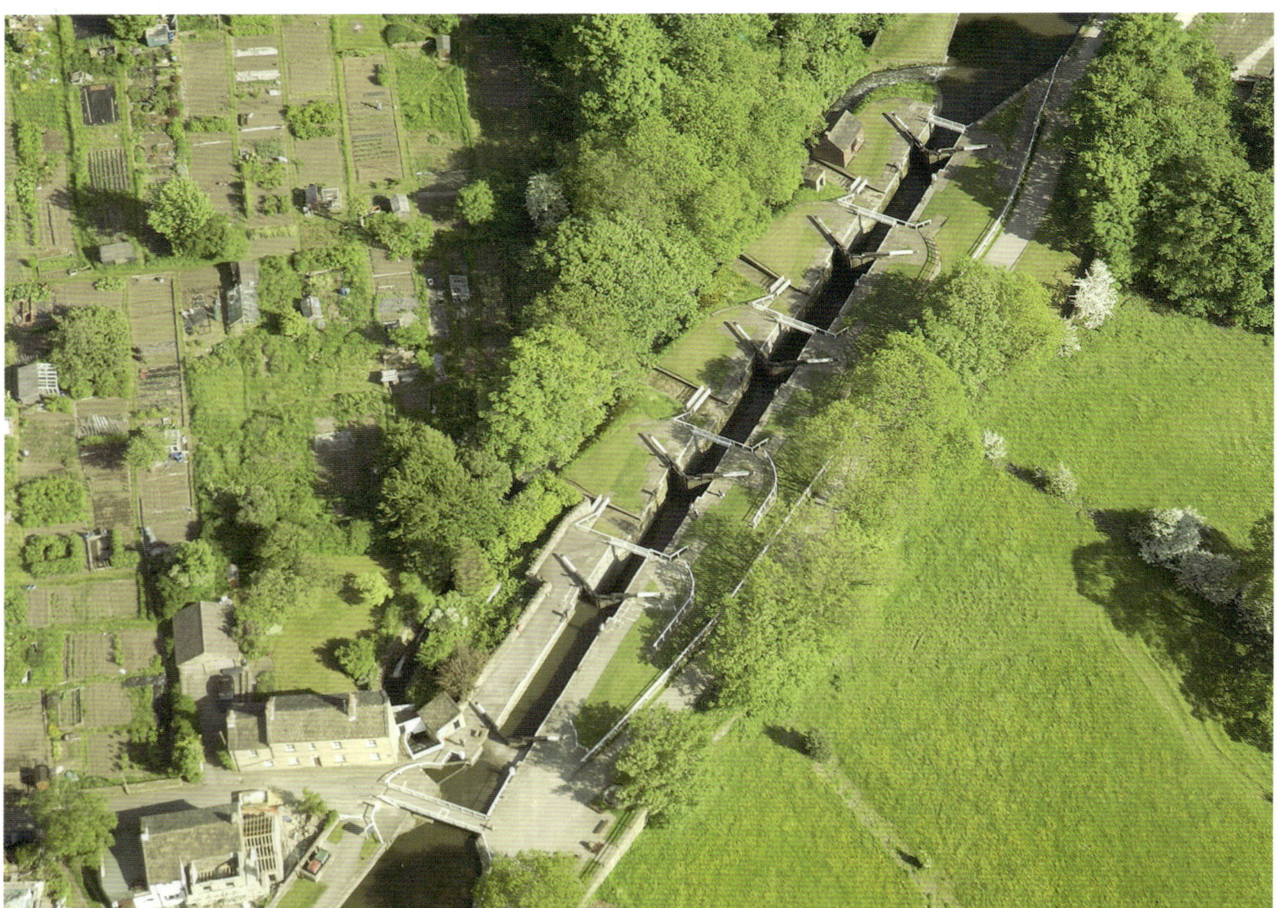

BINGLEY FIVE RISE LOCKS *(above)*

These locks are on the Leeds and Liverpool Canal which crosses the Pennines and therefore involved the frequent use of locks to ascend or descend steep slopes. On the Yorkshire side of the Pennines, as the canal rises out of Airedale there are, within a 16-mile stretch, three double locks, four staircase locks of three locks each and then the five-lock Bingley Rise. This set of locks, which raises the level of the canal by 59ft (18m), was originally called Bingley Great Lock. It was completed in 1777. In a staircase set of locks as at Bingley the top gate of one chamber acts as the bottom gate of the next chamber. Each chamber at Bingley can take a vessel 62ft (19m) long and just over 14ft (4.2m) wide.

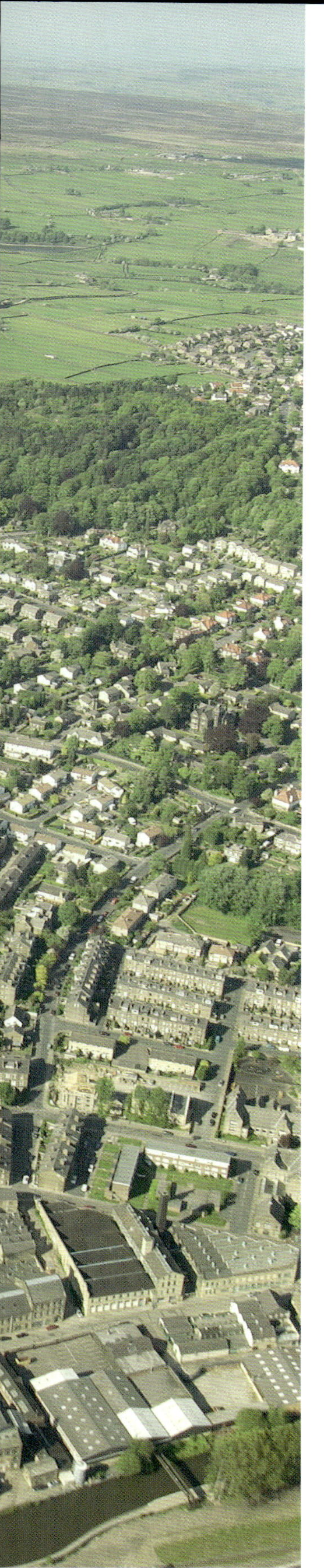

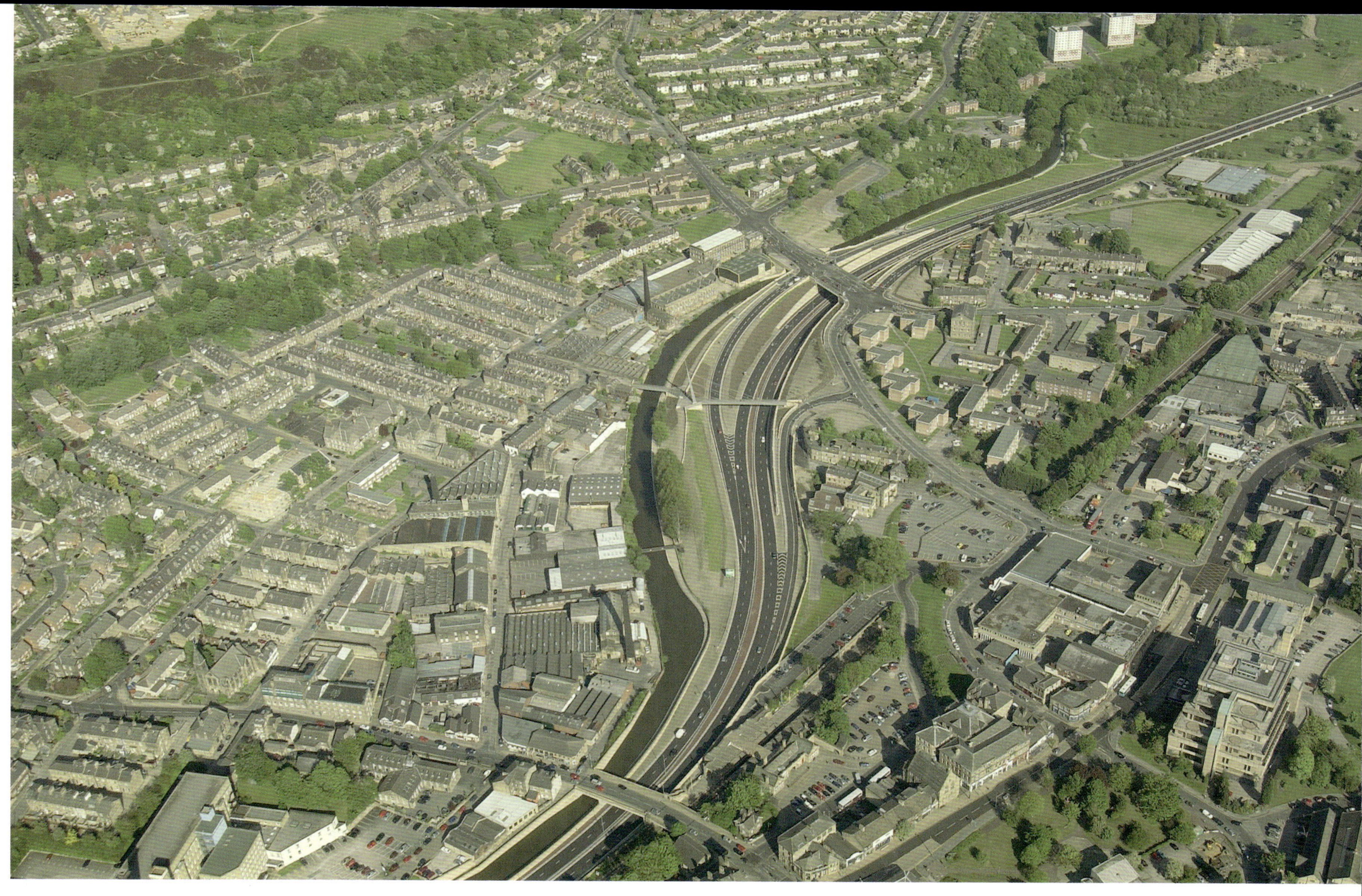

OTLEY *(below)*

Developed to the north and south of the river Wharfe halfway between Bradford and Ilkley, there are spectacular views of Otley from the Chevin, the gritstone escarpment to the south of the town that rises over 900ft (274m). Otley is a busy market town and the Otley Show began in 1796. It has two splendid churches, one medieval and the other late Victorian. The medieval church is All Saints parish church and the Victorian church is the Congregational church constructed in 1899. The photograph shows Otley Bridge over the river Wharfe.

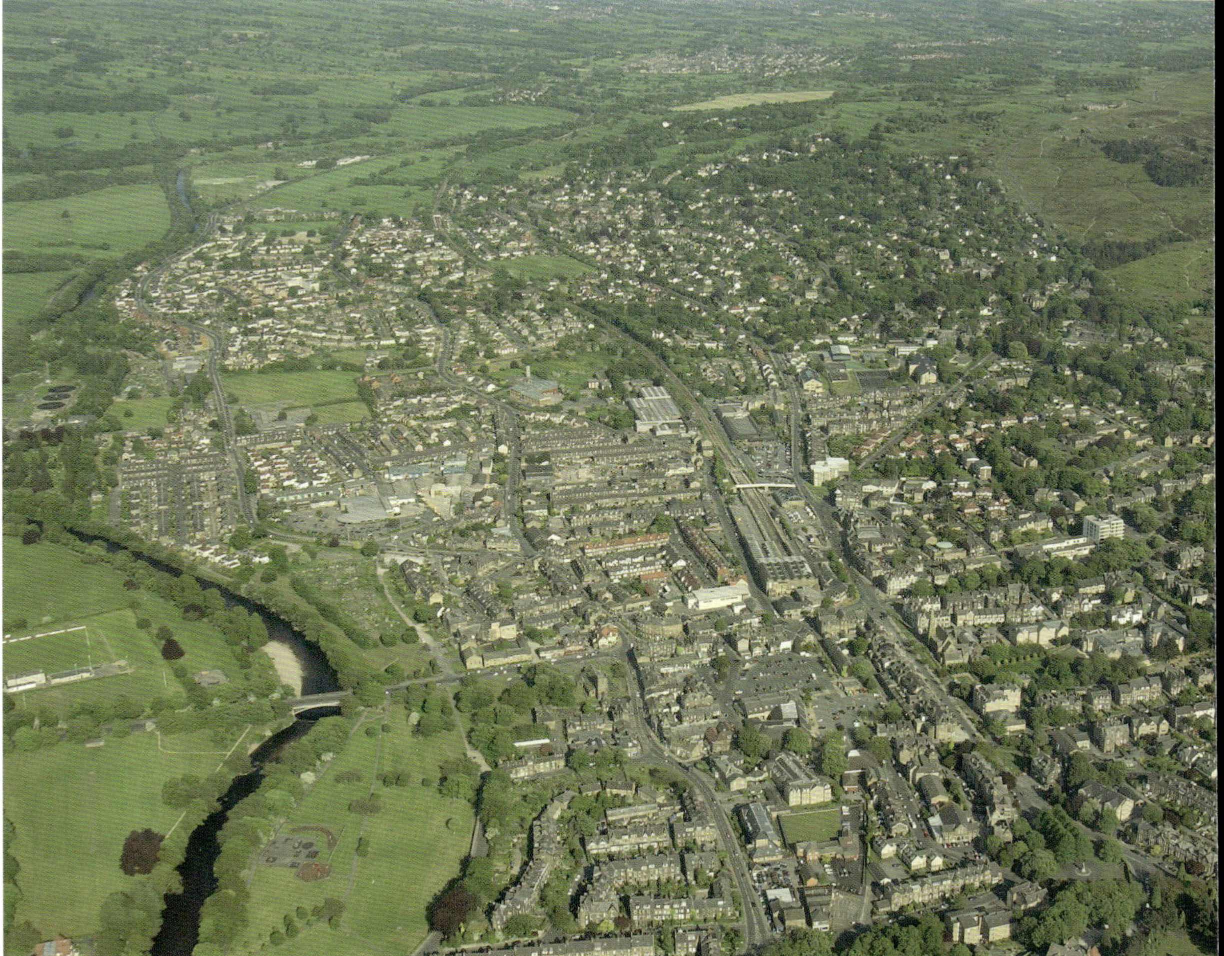

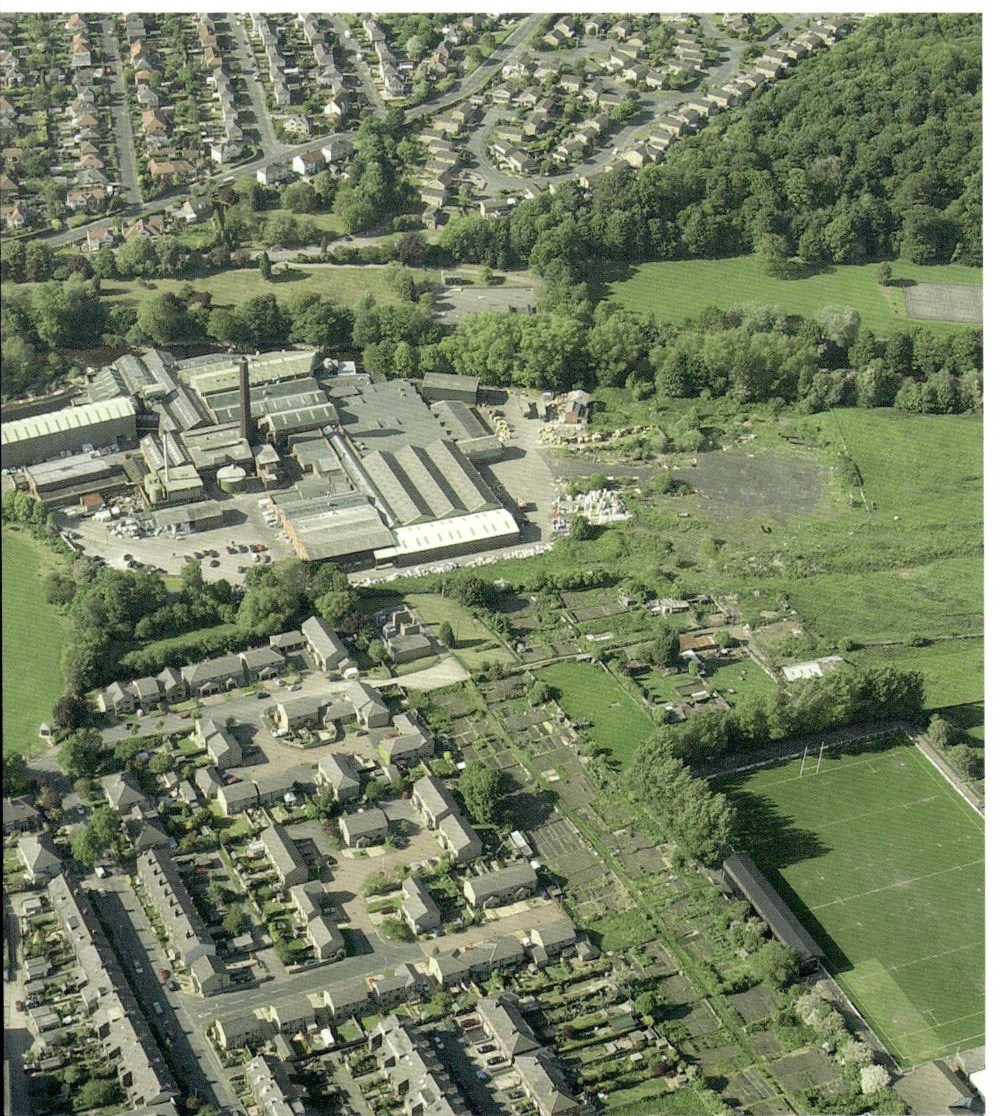

ILKLEY *(above)*

Ilkley is a pleasant commuter town in Wharfedale on the southern edge of the Yorkshire Dales. It hosts the Ilkley Literary Festival and the Ilkley Music Festival. It is also the starting point for the Dales Way long-distance footpath. The town rose to prominence in the 19th century as a spa town ("the Malvern of the north") and a number of purpose-built hydropathic hotels were built, the most well-known being Ben Rhydding, Craiglands, Troutbeck and Wells House. Wells House, which opened in 1856, was designed by Cuthbert Brodrick, the architect of Leeds Town Hall. One famous visitor to Ilkley in the autumn of 1859 was the naturalist Sir Charles Darwin awaiting the publication of his controversial *On the Origin of Species*, and suffering from stomach pains, swellings and boils. With the arrival of the railway in 1865 Ilkley entered its heyday as a fashionable resort and residential outpost for the successful industrialists, merchants and professional men of Leeds and Bradford. The town contains some notable Victorian and Edwardian buildings both public and private. These include the town hall in the Palladian style built between 1906-08; the railway station constructed in the Classical style in 1864; and private mansions by Richard Norman Shaw and Edwin Lutyens.

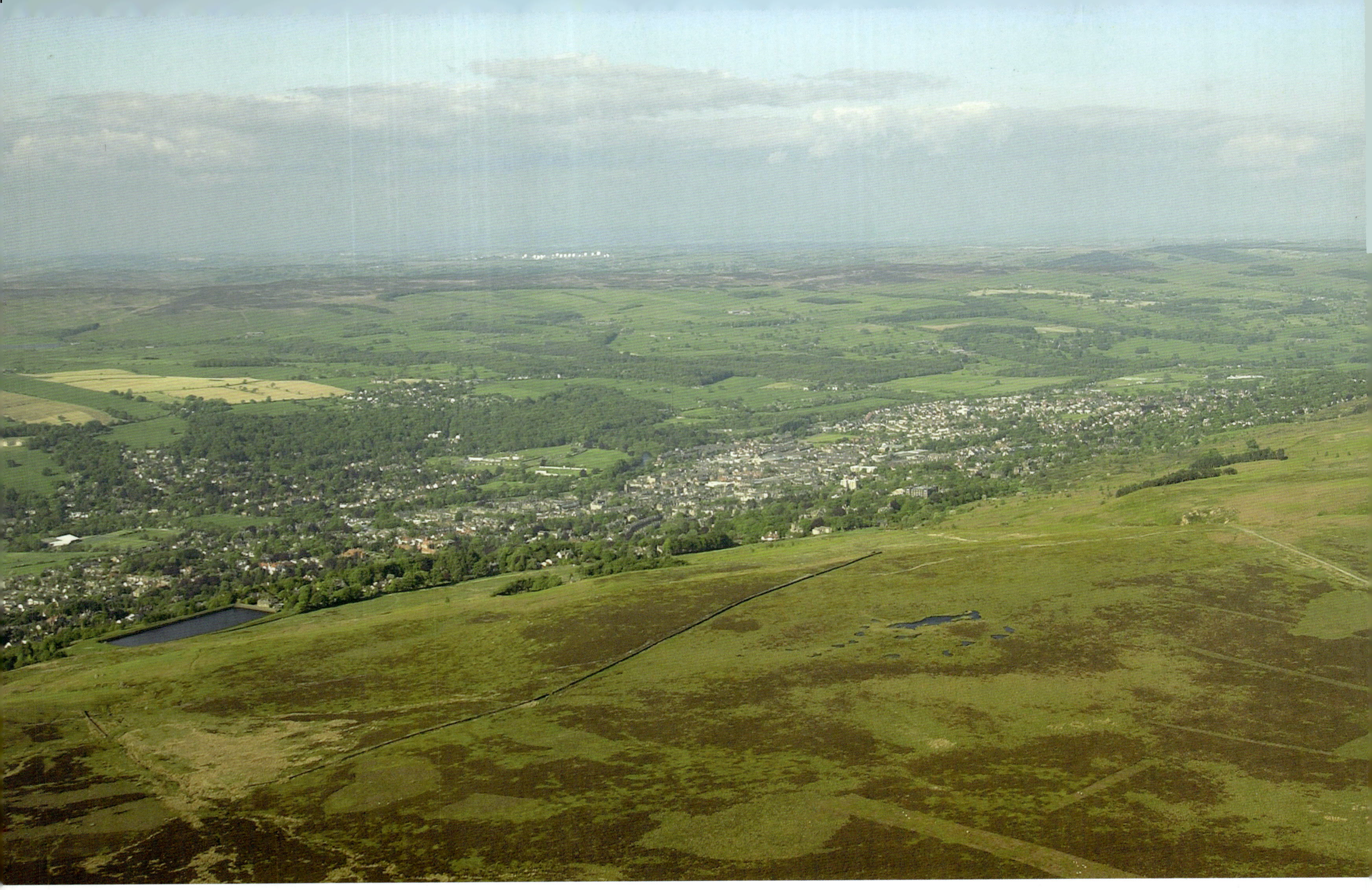

ILKLEY *(above)* AND THE COW AND CALF ROCKS ON ILKLEY MOOR *(right)*

Rising above the town of Ilkley to the south is Ilkley Moor, part of the much more extensive Rombalds Moor, rising to over 1,300ft (396m) with its gaunt millstone grit outcrops and glorious views of Wharfedale. It is also rich in prehistoric archaeological remains including cairns, barrows, hut circles and enigmatic "cup and ring" carvings in the millstone grit outcrops. Ilkley Moor has long been a mecca for excursionists, walkers and climbers from the industrial West Riding and the name is enshrined in the Yorkshire anthem *On Ilkla Mooar bah't 'at*. This is a tongue-in-cheek mocking song made up by members of a church choir outing about one of their members who had left the main party and gone out on the moor without his hat to court Mary Jane. It is sung to the hymn tune *Cranbrook* composed by Thomas Clark in 1808, but the words were not sung to the *Cranbrook* tune before the 1870s.

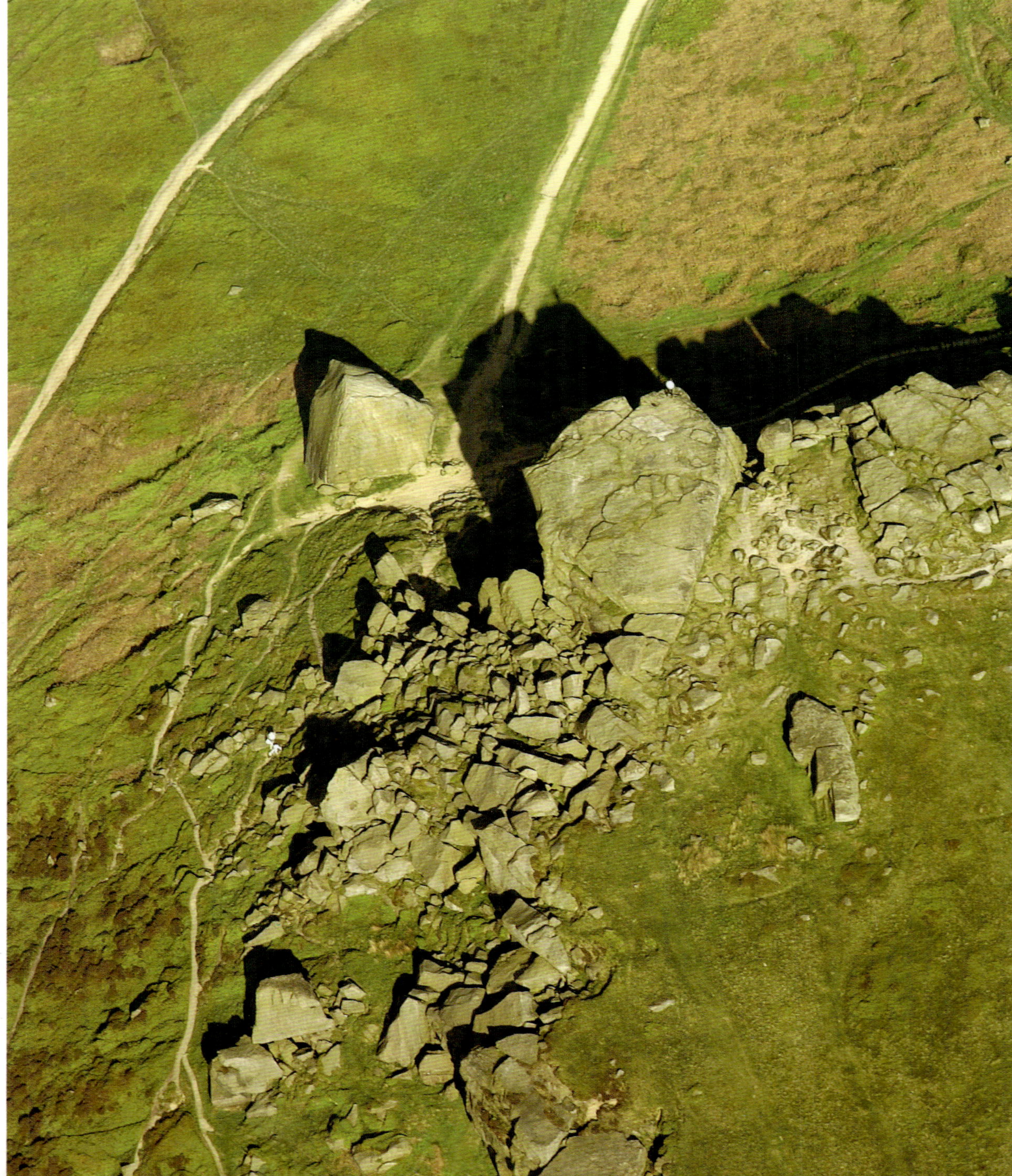

First published in 2006 by
Myriad Books Limited
35 Bishopsthorpe Road, London
SE26 4PA

Photographs © Ian Hay,
Flight Images

ISBN 1 904 736 580

Designed by Jerry Goldie
Printed in China

www.myriadbooks.com